ANGUS

G000017115

Discovering
Parish Boundaries

SHIRE PUBLICATIONS LTD

Contents

Cover: Boundary stone between Ingleton and Bentham parishes, North Yorkshire, near Nutgill Farm (SD 693 702).

Acknowledgement is made to Valerie Winchester for drawing the maps; to Lord Egremont and the Keeper of the Public Records for permission to reproduce photographs of manuscripts in their possession as plates 6 and 8, respectively; and to Mr Barker and the Local Studies Department of Shropshire County Library for permission to use the photograph reproduced as plate 9. Other photographs are by the author.

Note. The county names and areas referred to in this book are those which applied before the local government reorganisation of 1974.

British Library Cataloguing in Publication Data: Winchester, Angus J. L. Discovering parish boundaries. (Discovering series). 1. Great Britain. Parishes. Boundaries, history. I. Title. 941. ISBN 0-7478-0060-X.

Printed in Great Britain by C. I. Thomas & Sons (Haverfordwest) Ltd, Press Buildings, Merlins Bridge, Haverfordwest, Dyfed SA61 1XF.

1. Introduction

Anyone who has pored over one of the Ordnance Survey's old One Inch maps or the excellent 2½ inch 'Pathfinder' series is likely to have found their eyes following the dotted lines which mark the boundaries of civil parishes and other units of local administration. Snaking across the British countryside, following hedgerows, roads, footpaths, streams and rivers, or cutting across the landscape with no apparent reference to the lie of the land or to features of the human landscape, parish boundaries create a pattern of considerable complexity and raise numerous questions to the inquiring mind. Why does a boundary which has been following a particular stream suddenly swing away to follow lanes and hedgerows for a couple of miles before rejoining the stream on its course to the sea? Why was a Roman road used to mark the limits of parishes in one area but totally ignored by the boundaries a few miles further on? Why do parishes vary so much in shape and size between different parts of the country?

This intriguing pattern has received considerable attention from people studying the history of the British landscape since the 1960s. Archaeologists and local historians have become aware that the network of territorial boundaries has generally been a stable element in the landscape and that many boundary lines are of great antiquity. Now that we are revising our views of the timelessness of the English village, for example, and are beginning to realise that rural settlement has undergone a steady process of change in which the position of villages, farmsteads and cottages has shifted across the countryside, it is to the territorial framework that we turn to seek some of the oldest features in the English countryside. The dotted lines on the Ordnance Survey maps are in some, perhaps many, cases among the most durable legacies from Anglo-Saxon England.

Once established, the network of parish boundaries formed an invisible web which both bound families into communities and divided communities one from another. The landscape of local administration was both ecclesiastical (determining the church in which a person was baptised and buried and to which he paid tithes and other dues) and civil (dictating the official to whom he was responsible for payment of taxes and rates, for example). The boundaries of parishes and other units of local administration mattered greatly to our ancestors. Before the local government reforms of the nineteenth century, the parochial basis of poor relief and many charities and schools gave considerable importance to the parish in which a person was born and thus endowed parish boundaries with, perhaps, undue significance. In his diary for 1870 the Reverend Francis

INTRODUCTION

Kilvert described a house straddling the Welsh border on the edge of Brilley parish, Herefordshire. The line of the parish boundary through the house was marked by a notch in the chimney and he recalled hearing the story of the lengths to which a midwife once went to ensure that a baby was born in the English part of the house, making the mother give birth standing in a corner!

A substantial body of work on parish and other territorial boundaries, much of it local, has appeared in print in recent years but most of it is buried in specialist journals and is thus comparatively inaccessible. The difficulty of finding the fruits of recent research is compounded by the rather baffling array of medieval terms and concepts with which the local historian is confronted as soon as he begins to examine parish boundaries in any depth. This book is therefore conceived as a practical hand-book: a guide to where to start a study of local territorial boundaries, what questions to ask, and how to assess the significance of a particular boundary pattern in historical and archaeological terms.

The following pages introduce the terminology and historical background to the parish and other local territorial divisions found in England, Wales and Scotland and summarise the current state of knowledge about the origins and development of these administrative units and their boundaries. A guide to further reading has also been included in the hope that this brief introduction will stimulate the reader to explore an important aspect of local history in greater depth.

2. What is a parish?

If it were to occur in a game of word association, the word 'parish' would probably bring either the word 'church' or 'priest' to the mind of the next player: the parish is firmly fixed in our minds as a religious entity, associated with the rhythm of life and the annual round of church celebrations — baptisms, marriages and burials; Easter communion, harvest festivals and carol services. When we examine the parish as an institution, however, and ask what is signified by its boundaries, it is important to remember that the term 'parish' has been used of two quite distinct units of administration since 1889, the *civil parish* on the one hand, and the *ecclesiastical parish* on the other. It is the boundaries of the civil parishes which are portrayed on modern large-scale Ordnance Survey maps, not those of their ecclesiastical namesakes, though, as we shall see, civil parish and ecclesiastical parish could and often did coincide.

The civil parish is the bottom rung of the local government hierarchy, a territory governed by a parish council which has authority to levy a small rate to provide such amenities as playing fields, allotment gardens, street lighting and bus shelters. The term, a misnomer which has led to much confusion, originated in the local government reforms of the nineteenth century. The Local Government Act of 1889 defined the civil parish as 'a place for which a separate poor rate is or can be made', referring back to the system of poor law administration which originated under the Tudors. The Tudor Poor Law acts laid responsibility for the poor with the ancient *ecclesiastical* parish, thus giving a civil function to the ecclesiastical unit. The Settlement Act of 1662, however, allowed large parishes to be divided for poor law purposes into their constituent 'townships or villages', and in parts of England, particularly in the northern counties, it was the ancient secular administrative unit, the *township* or *vill*, rather than the ancient ecclesiastical parish, which had responsibility for raising poor rates and thus became the civil parish of the later nineteenth century. In their monumental survey of legal institutions Pollock and Maitland (1923) concluded that 'in general the vill of the thirteenth century is the "civil parish" of the nineteenth'.

The history of the civil parish is an example of one of the principal themes in the history of territorial units in Britain, namely that a new unit of local administration is generally defined in terms of an existing local government unit. The legislators of 1889 used the units of poor law administration which had themselves been defined in terms of older medieval units, the parish and vill. It is because of this that the network of civil

5

parish boundaries is often such an ancient and stable pattern in the landscape. Since the 1889 Act the old pattern of local government boundaries inherited from the medieval period has been tinkered with and in places completely rewritten to create civil parishes appropriate to modern conditions. This is particularly true where urban growth has made earlier administrative units redundant and it is important when studying boundaries in a local area to recapture the pattern as it existed before these modern changes. This can usually be done most simply by taking the earliest Ordnance Survey Six Inch (1:10,560) maps as a starting point, and it is useful to remember that civil parish boundary changes in each decade are detailed in each of the published census reports. The townships and vills of medieval England, the local communities as defined for such purposes as the collection of taxes and the administration of law and order, are examined in greater detail in chapter 4.

The confusion between the civil parish and the ecclesiastical parish arises because the relationship between the two units has varied both across the country and across time. In many parts of the rural south and Midlands the ecclesiastical parish and the civil unit have been one and the same stretch of land, whereas the two units were often of quite different orders of magnitude in the north. Furthermore, as a result of the proliferation of Anglican churches in the middle decades of the nineteenth century and, conversely, the amalgamation of livings into larger parishes in recent decades, the modern ecclesiastical parish is often a unit of no great antiquity and we have to delve behind the reorganisations of Church of England parishes since the 1830s in order to recapture the pattern inherited from the middle ages. In this book the term 'parish' will henceforth be used to refer to the *ancient ecclesiastical parish* which was the basic unit of church organisation before the nineteenth century. It may be defined as a community served by a priest in a parish church and supporting that priest by the payment of tithes and other dues. As the practice of paying tithe originated in the Anglo-Saxon period, the parish acquired a territorial dimension early, its boundaries being those of the lands of the parish community from which its priest could claim tithes. Civil duties, notably those of maintaining highways and relieving the poor, were imposed on the parish by the Tudors so that many of the small parishes of southern England, particularly when they corresponded to a single vill, were the units which became civil parishes in the nineteenth century. How the ancient parish came into being and what factors determined its boundaries are considered in more detail in chapter 3.

The relationship of the ancient ecclesiastical parish to the township or vill differed between the northern and southern

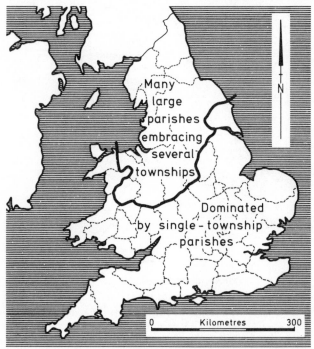

Figure 1. Dorothy Sylvester's 'parish line'. (After Sylvester, 1969.)

counties of England, as we have seen. The pattern on the eve of the nineteenth-century changes is captured in the published Enumeration Abstracts of the early nineteenth-century censuses and has led Dorothy Sylvester to identify a 'parish line', dividing the northern counties, in which most parishes were large and contained several townships, from the southern counties, where single-township parishes predominated (see figure 1). The contrast between different counties was striking: 85 per cent of Gloucestershire's parishes contained just a single township, compared with only fifteen of Lancashire's 68 parishes, almost a third of which embraced more than seven townships (Sylvester, 1969). Some northern parishes covered vast territories. Those which stretched up into the moors and fells were among the largest: Whalley parish (Lancashire), for example, embraced no fewer than 47 townships and over 105,000 acres (43,000 ha); Kendal parish (Westmorland), 25 townships and 68,360 acres

7

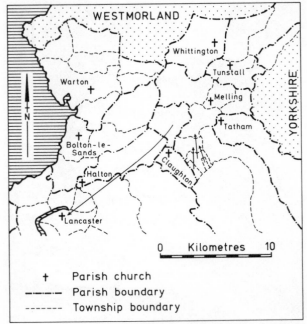

Figure 2. Parish and township boundaries in northern Lancashire.

(27,665 ha). Even lowland parishes could be extensive in the north: the parish of Kirkham in the Fylde of Lancashire contained seventeen townships and almost 44,000 acres (18,000 ha). At the local level, however, large and small parishes were often found side by side, as in the Lune valley in north Lancashire (figure 2), and even in areas dominated by single-township parishes the occasional multi-township parish is found.

This book is dealing principally, then, with two quite separate historical patterns, the division of the countryside into townships for secular purposes on the one hand, and the pattern of ancient ecclesiastical parish boundaries on the other. The modern map of civil parishes is, as we have seen, an amalgam of the two patterns, depending on whether it was township or ancient parish that was taken as the unit for the administration of the Tudor poor law. The following two chapters try to disentangle the two sets of territories, asking for each how, when, why and by whom the boundaries delineated on the early Ordnance Survey maps came to be fixed.

3. The ancient parish

As we have seen, the ancient parish was the community which, by payment of tithes and other obligations such as Easter dues, supported a priest in a parish church, who in turn was responsible for the 'cure of souls', that is the spiritual needs, of all the inhabitants within the parish community. The payment of tithes to the church was made obligatory in England in the tenth century under the laws of Edmund (in AD 939-46) and Edgar (in 970), and the land paying tithes to a particular church came to be that church's parish territory. Not all churches were parish churches. Where a parish embraced several rural communities, subsidiary churches, known as chapels of ease, were often built to serve outlying settlements. They were buildings in which services were held but which lacked the institutional independence of the parish church. They were often served by a poorly paid curate employed by the parish priest; they generally had no burial ground of their own; and the community for which they were built continued to pay tithes to the parish priest and to be buried at the parish church. Many chapels of ease were raised to the status of parish churches in their own right in the reforms of the nineteenth century but for the purposes of this discussion we are concerned only with the ancient (that is pre-nineteenth-century) parishes.

In general the network of boundaries dividing the tithe-paying territories of different parish churches remained stable from the thirteenth century until the spate of parish creation which started in the 1830s. For most of England and Wales the earliest list of parishes is provided by the Papal Taxation of 1291 (published in 1802 by the Record Commission under the title *Taxatio Ecclesiastica Angliae et Walliae, auctoritate Papae Nicholai IV, circa 1291*). It suggests that there were about nine thousand parishes in England by the end of the thirteenth century, and a comparison with a listing of parish churches in a local area in the early nineteenth century (from the Census Enumeration Abstracts for 1811 or 1831, for example) often shows little change since 1291. The reason for this remarkable stability was the jealousy with which parish priests (and, equally importantly, their successors as tithe owners in parishes which were appropriated by monastic houses) guarded their right to take tithe: the establishment of a new parish would necessarily reduce the tithe income of an existing living. There are nevertheless scattered examples all over the country of chapels which were elevated to parish church status and, conversely, of churches which slipped into the role of dependent chapels. The tendency to raise chapels to parish churches by carving them a section of their mother church's parish was particularly common

9

in the vast parishes of northern England. Grasmere and Windermere parishes (Westmorland) were carved out of the massive parish of Kendal in the fourteenth century. Hawkshead (Lancashire), a chapel in the medieval parish of Dalton-in-Furness, was made a parish after the Reformation and was later itself divided, its southern half becoming the parish of Colton in 1676. The dismemberment of Croston parish (Lancashire), which embraced ten townships, began with the elevation of the chapelry of Much Hoole into a separate parish in 1642, though other townships did not gain independence until the creation of new parishes in 1793, 1821 and 1840. Where there were numerous small parishes by 1300, in later centuries poor livings were sometimes absorbed into their wealthy neighbours. In 1432, for example, the parish of West Lee (Essex) was considered too poor to support its own priest and was effectively united with the neighbouring parish of Langdon; in the same century the parish of Buncton (Sussex) was absorbed into Ashington parish. Sometimes the change in status was only temporary: Ashingdon (Essex) was united with Hawkwell parish in 1429 but was separated again in 1457 and the livings remained separate; Dawley (Shropshire), a separate parish in the thirteenth century, was considered to be a chapel of Shifnal parish from 1256 to 1563, after which it was independent again. These examples, drawn at random from the pages of the Victoria County Histories, are the exceptions: most parishes in existence in the early nineteenth century were also recorded in 1291.

Parish origins

If we can trace the parochial pattern back largely unchanged to the later thirteenth century, we must look to the Anglo-Saxon period and the first century or so after the Norman Conquest to chart the processes by which the pattern of parish boundaries came into being. Late Saxon documents distinguish between *minster* churches or 'mother churches', ancient churches served by a group of clergy who ministered to the population of a very large area, and 'field churches', lesser and often more recent churches which had their own graveyards. The story of the English parish is generally told in terms of these two generations of church foundation, with the tenth-century tithe laws speeding the definition of hard boundaries between church territories. The minster churches were generally royal or episcopal foundations established in the seventh or eighth centuries, often close to important estate centres. They were founded to serve either the estate on which they were placed or a broader region, the *regio* or *provincia,* the area occupied by a particular tribal group. Evidence that a church originated as a minster comes from various sources. In some places the term 'minster' survives in a place-name to record the presence of such a church (for example Kidderminster, Wimborne Minster); in others the existence of 'portions', where a parish living was held by more than one priest, survives as a memory of the group of clergy serving a minster's territory in Anglo-Saxon times; or monetary payments ('pensions') from neighbouring parishes may record the former dependence of lesser churches which had been carved out of a minster's territory. In many cases churches for which there is evidence of an early foundation continued to possess large parishes, extending over several surrounding settlements, in the medieval period (Addleshaw, 1953; Bettey, 1987).

The majority of English parish churches originated as lesser churches founded by lay landowners on their estates mainly in the two centuries between AD 950 and 1150. These 'seigniorial' churches, established in the period when tithe payment was rapidly becoming formalised as the principal source of income for parish clergy, came to be endowed with the tithes from the founder's estate and resulted in new parishes being carved out of the earlier, and probably rather vaguer, territory belonging to a minster church. The fact that so many of the new generation of parish churches were founded by landowners is important: such a church was often first and foremost an estate church and the boundaries of its parish generally bore some relationship to those of its founder's property. The contrast in the size and pattern of medieval parishes between northern and southern England is probably a reflection of variations in the amount of seigniorial church foundation in different parts of the country in the centuries either side of the Norman Conquest. A combination of circumstances would have led to these regional differences, including greater wealth and population density in the south and a stronger tradition of church foundation among southern lords of the manor on the one hand and the continuing importance of overlordship and large 'multiple' estates in the north, where the larger parishes of 'mother churches' often survived, on the other. There was also a contrast in southern England between east and west. Seigniorial foundations appear to have reached their fullest extent in East Anglia, where many settlements possessed more than one parish church, each serving a separate estate.

Factors influencing parish shape and size

By the thirteenth century there was thus a wide spectrum of parish size and shape across England. At one extreme were the vast multi-township parishes of the north; at the other were the small parishes whose territories covered only part of a township. In the middle were the majority of parishes, where the church's tithe-paying territory coincided exactly or approximately with the land of a single township or vill. In these numerous cases the parish may be thought of as having 'borrowed' the boundaries of the vill and we shall explore how the boundaries of the latter came to be defined in the following chapter. What is to be examined here are those cases where parish and township did not coincide. What determined that a particular township should lie in one parish rather than another? How do we explain those parishes which consisted largely of scattered, fragmented pieces of land?

To explore these questions let us examine the pattern of parish boundaries in four local areas. The first is the Wellington area of Telford in Shropshire (figure 3). It contained four ancient parishes: Wellington, embracing twelve complete townships and parts of three more; Wrockwardine, containing six townships together with a detached block of land called Wrockwardine Wood; and the two small parishes of Eyton and Pres-

Figure 3. Parish and township boundaries around Wellington, Shropshire (SJ 61). (After VCH Shropshire, volume XI).

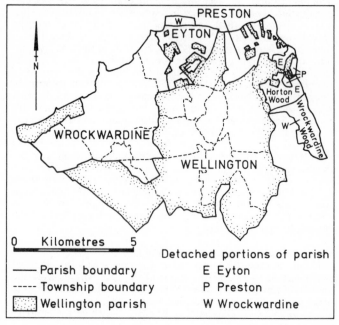

12

ton. These were each centred on a township in which Wellington parish also had land, and each also included detached portions near Wrockwardine Wood. It is a pattern of some complexity: two multi-township parishes intermingled with two very small parishes. The development of the parochial pattern in the area illustrates several themes which surface again and again when seeking explanations for parish boundaries. First is the importance of large Anglo-Saxon estates as the focus for large early parishes. Both Wrockwardine and Wellington were the centres of large estates in 1066. The former contained 7½ 'berewicks' (outlying settlements) and may have been a very early royal state; the latter contained five berewicks. The churches of both parishes were mentioned in Domesday Book and it seems likely that both may be seen, if not as minster churches in the strict sense of the word, at least as early churches founded at important estate centres. A second theme has already been introduced, namely the tension between old and new livings when a new parish was carved out of an earlier church's territory. Eyton and Preston originated as chapels of ease within Wellington parish. Both had become independent by the fourteenth century but a proportion of the tithes of each township (in Eyton's case one-third) was retained by Wellington parish. Originally the division of the tithes in this way was probably achieved by a transfer in kind or in money representing a share of the tithes from the whole township, but during the eighteenth century a territorial division of Eyton and Preston townships was made, so that certain fields were considered to lie in Wellington parish, and others in the parishes of Eyton and Preston. The complicated intermingling of two parishes in these townships is thus to be seen as an eighteenth-century formalisation of medieval tithe-paying practice. A third theme is the influence of rights on intercommoned woodland and waste in creating detached portions of parishes. The detached parts of Wrockwardine, Eyton and Preston parishes in a belt down the eastern side of the area under discussion represent a late-surviving block of woodland, the existence of which is recorded in the names Wrockwardine Wood and Horton Wood. The rights of the communities of Eyton, Preston and Wrockwardine needed clarification in 1238 and we may assume that the parish boundaries in this area of former woodland reflect its division between the three manors in the thirteenth century (*VCH Shropshire*, volume XI).

Our second and third examples also concern parishes which included numerous small detached portions. The parishes of Somerton and Charlton Adam in Somerset (figure 4) both consisted of a compact nucleus of land together with outlying small detached pieces, but their origins were very different. Somerton

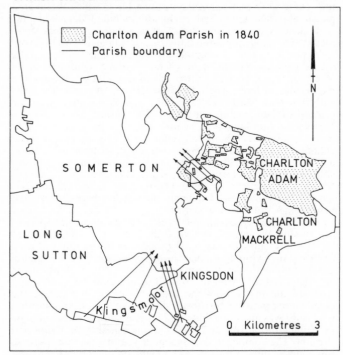

Figure 4. Somerton area, Somerset (ST 42/52): ancient parishes. (After VCH Somerset, volume III.)

was an important and early royal estate centre and has been claimed to be the 'ancient capital of Wessex'. Its church was probably an early mother church for the estate, which subsequently lost territory to newer foundations in neighbouring settlements. The detached portions reflect Somerton's earlier rights over a larger area than the medieval parish: the fragments in Kingsdon being a reminder that Kingsdon was a constituent part of Somerton manor until the twelfth century; the pieces of Somerton parish along the southern edge of Long Sutton and Kingsdon representing Somerton's share in Kingsmoor, an area of wetland enclosed in 1795. Again, it should be noted that the parish boundaries in Kingsmoor were finally defined only at enclosure. The detached pieces of Somerton parish may thus be thought of, ultimately, as reminders of the extensive influence of a Saxon royal estate. Charlton Adam, on the other hand, reflects the pattern of landownership in the thirteenth and four-teenth centuries. The two Charltons presumably represent the division into two estates of an original settlement called Charlton. Charlton Adam, the compact block of the parish in the north-east corner of Charlton Mackrell parish, was granted by William son of Adam to Bruton Priory in 1258. The num-erous small detached portions which make up the rest of Charlton Adam parish probably originated as additional grants of land to the priory over the following century, which came to be accounted parts of the manor and thus the parish of Charlton Adam (*VCH Somerset*, volume III).

The parishes of Westcott Barton and Steeple Barton in Oxfordshire (figure 5) are an example of the division of a single village into two parishes. The division had occurred before 1066 but the two parishes continued to share a single field system. The pattern of parish boundaries illustrated in figure 5 appears to be a rationalisation of an even more complex earlier pattern. The enclosure award of 1796 confirmed the existence of six detached pieces of Steeple Barton parish in Westcott Barton but thirty years earlier there had been 48 such detached portions in Westcott Barton which paid tithe to the neighbouring parish (*VCH Oxfordshire*, volume XI). The Bartons appear to be an example of a fairly common phenomenon in parts of southern England, where two parishes, probably originating in seigniorial church foundations in the tenth or eleventh cen-turies, shared the tithes from a single field system. Perhaps the most extreme cases of such village sharing are found in East Anglia. Peter Warner has shown that, in Norfolk alone, there are 37 known examples of two or more parish churches sharing one churchyard. He suggests that this proliferation of churches was the result not only of church foundation by lords of the manor but of church building by communities of freemen during the eleventh century (Warner, 1986). The parishes thus created often consisted of scattered pieces in the open fields and, as in the Bartons in Oxfordshire, consolidation and rationalisation of the parochial boundary pattern in the eighteenth and nineteenth centuries has often reduced the complexity of earlier arrange-ments.

The final example is not of fragmented parishes but of large parishes embracing several townships. Figure 6 shows the pat-tern of parish boundaries in west Cumberland, an area in which the narrow strip of lowland along the coast gives way abruptly to the mountainous terrain of the Lake District. The pattern of parish boundaries mirrors this landscape contrast, the coastal lowlands containing numerous small parishes, some of which consist of only one township, while the western valleys of the Lake District were parcelled out between the three vast parishes

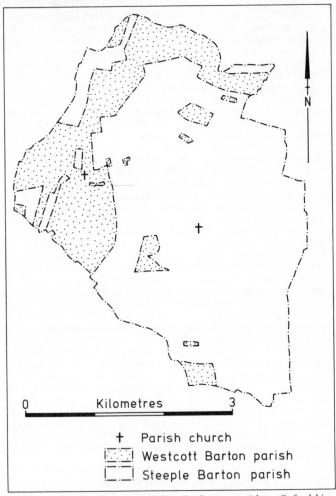

Figure 5. Westcott Barton and Steeple Barton parishes, Oxfordshire (SP 42). (After VCH Oxfordshire, volume XI.)

of Brigham, St Bees and Millom. The pattern also reflects very closely the pattern of lordship in the twelfth century. The area then consisted of three large baronial estates, centred on castles

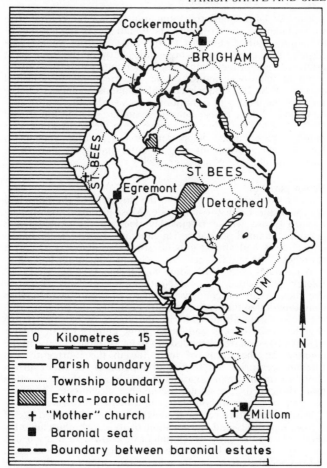

Figure 6. West Cumberland: parishes and townships.

at Cockermouth, Egremont and Millom, in each of which there was a clear division between a manorialised lowland in which most townships were manors in their own rights, and the Lake District uplands which were retained in the overlords' hands as private forest. The parochial pattern may be interpreted as consisting of three 'mother' churches (Brigham, St Bees and Millom), each associated with one of the three great estates, and a string of later seigniorial foundations down the coastal strip with smaller parish territories. The boundaries of the parishes of the three mother churches in the Lake District valleys correspond very closely to the boundaries between the three great estates, Brigham including most settlements within the private forest of the Cockermouth estate, the great upland detached portion of St Bees parish coinciding almost exactly with the forest of the barony of Egremont as it existed in the twelfth century, and Millom parish bearing a similar relationship to the lordship of Millom. Here, as elsewhere in the north where vast parishes were found, the pattern of overlordship appears to have played a dominant role in determining the pattern of parish boundaries (Winchester, 1987).

Urban parishes

So far we have looked at the development of the parochial system in the English countryside. Most medieval towns, particularly those whose origins lay deep in the Anglo-Saxon period, contained several parish churches. Indeed, some of the larger towns had almost unbelievably large numbers of parish churches in the middle ages: Norwich and Winchester had about sixty churches each; York some 46; Lincoln 35; Canterbury 22; Exeter 19; Oxford 17; and Northampton perhaps 11 parish churches. As in the countryside, many of these town churches were founded in the tenth to twelfth centuries, the process slowing down after about 1150 as the rights of existing parish churches over burials and tithes were enforced with greater rigidity. Town churches tended not to be as stable as those in the countryside: the decay of town life in the fourteenth and fifteenth centuries led to the disappearance of many urban churches or the amalgamation of parishes, so that it is often more difficult to reconstruct the number of churches, let alone the pattern of parish boundaries in a medieval town.

Where the pattern can be reconstructed, the shape and size of a town's parishes and the location of its parish churches may shed light on the early development of a town. In many towns there was a contrast between churches whose parishes extended out beyond the urban precincts to include often extensive tracts of countryside and those churches whose much smaller parishes lay entirely within the town walls. The larger parishes with extra-mural lands are generally interpreted as being the earliest foundations, the small intra-mural parishes being seen as later foundations which were unable to wrest tithes from farmland outside the town from established parish churches. Detailed discussions of the development of parochial boundaries in early towns are to be found in Campbell, 1979; Rogers, 1972; and Williams, 1982.

4. Township and tithing

As we have seen, in many places, particularly in the southern and Midland counties of England, a block of land was both a parish and a vill, and the boundaries of the parish were those of the vill community. In northern counties, where a parish extended over several vills, the boundaries of those vills have usually come down to us as the bounds of modern 'civil parishes'. The tithing was the southern English counterpart of the vill in some areas and in others a much more shadowy unit which barely survived the medieval period. How do we begin to interpret the pattern created by the boundaries of these basic civil divisions of the English countryside?

Township, vill and tithing

The terms 'township' and 'vill' are so closely related that they are often used synonymously, though the tradition among legal historians has been to use 'township' to refer to the rural community as defined for the purposes of fiscal and judicial administration, and 'vill' to refer to the tract of land. Medieval Latin distinguished between the two, *villa* being used of the territory and *villata* of the community. Both, however, are derived from the same English root, 'town', used of the basic unit of settlement and community: as late as the seventeenth century we find references to the inhabitants of 'the town of X', where in modern usage we would use the terms 'village' or 'civil parish' of X.

The administrative landscape of the post-medieval north of England was often rather more complicated than may have been implied by the simple distinction between parish on the one hand and township on the other. Constructing a map of townships in a northern county is not always a simple matter, as a tract of land which was a self-contained unit for one administrative purpose was sometimes part of a larger unit for another (see Winchester, 1978). Some parishes continued to maintain their poor as a whole, even when they were divided into two or more townships for other purposes, such as the upkeep of highways. Or townships were sometimes themselves divided into *hamlets* for highway maintenance. Conversely, the *chapelry* (an ecclesiastical division of the parish often embracing more than one township) sometimes surfaces as the dominant unit of civil administration in larger parishes. Another northern English phenomenon was the *quarter*, a subdivision of the parish usually appointing its own churchwarden and sometimes maintaining its own poor and highways, and even having its own constable. Some quarters coincided with a township or chapelry but others did not. In parts of the north one has almost to draw as many

19

separate maps of the local units of civil administration in the seventeenth and eighteenth centuries as there were different administrative functions! The complexity of the resulting patterns can probably be simplified by thinking of the quarter and chapelry as being essentially *subdivisions* of the ecclesiastical parish, overlying and sometimes cutting across the township structure which usually shines through as the basic building blocks of the secular administrative hierarchy.

The medieval vill was the basic unit of local administration, the unit with which the royal courts and tax collectors worked. It was the vill rather than the manor which formed the smallest unit for the assessment and collection of taxes, both for the assessment of geld (a tax related to the value of land) recorded in Domesday Book and (in most parts of England) for the collection of the fourteenth-century Lay Subsidies (a tax on the value of a man's movable goods). From the twelfth century onwards the vill was also the local peacekeeping unit, responsible for pursuing criminals and bringing them before the justices. For these purposes it was represented by its reeve and four men. Like the parish, the vill or township was essentially a community rather than a territory but a territorial dimension developed early through, for example, the vill's duty to chase suspects within its bounds. By the fifteenth century the lawyer Sir John Fortescue could write: 'there is scarcely any place in England that is not contained within the ambits of vills.' At its simplest the vill or township can thus be thought of as 'the village and its lands' and, in areas dominated by large villages, the boundaries between vills 'seem almost to draw themselves', as Maitland said. However, much of England possesses a much more scattered settlement pattern consisting of small hamlets and dispersed farmsteads. In these areas lordship or the existence of early local folk meetings were probably the forces which bound scattered groups of farms together into township communities. A hint of these early origins in the north of England comes in the term *bierlow* or *byerlaw*, a term which came to be almost synonymous with 'village community, township' and survived in place-names such as Brampton Bierlow, Brightside Bierlow and Eccleshall Bierlow in the West Riding of Yorkshire. Derived from the Scandinavian term *byjar-log*, meaning 'the local law of the township', it hints that a village meeting, a sort of proto-manor court making regulations affecting the whole community, was the essential feature binding scattered farms into a township community.

The township or vill is often portrayed as the ubiquitous unit of local administration in the medieval countryside. In the south of England, however, another unit, the *tithing*, replaced the vill as far as medieval royal administrators were concerned. The origins of the tithing lay in the Anglo-Saxon system of frankpledge by which, in theory, each hundred (see chapter 8) was divided into ten groups of men responsible for the capture of criminals. The equivalent grouping in Kent and Sussex was the *borgh*, an association of ten householders who stood pledge for each other in the maintenance of law and order. After the Conquest almost all members of the adult male population south, roughly, of the Humber-Severn line, were supposed to belong to a tithing, through which they were collectively responsible for catching suspects and bringing them to justice. In the south and west of England the tithing became the territorial equivalent of the vill, with the tithingman the counterpart of the township reeve. In these areas the tithing survived into the nineteenth century as the subdivision of the parish which further north would have been termed a township. Tithings in Wiltshire, for example, were assessed separately for the collection of taxes; each tithing

Figure 7. Collingbourne Kingston, Wiltshire (SU 25): tithing boundaries. (After Bonney, 1969.)

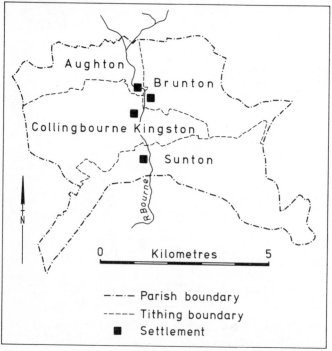

21

was responsible as a community for the upkeep of the roads within its bounds and was represented separately at the courts of Quarter Sessions. The 1831 Census Enumeration Abstracts show that tithings were the common subdivisions of parishes throughout Wessex from Berkshire, Surrey and Hampshire, through Wiltshire, Dorset and Gloucestershire, to Somerset and Devon.

Not all tithings survived to become civil parishes, however, as

Figure 8. Treleaver Tithing, Cornwall (SW 71/72). Reconstructed from information given in Pool, 1981.

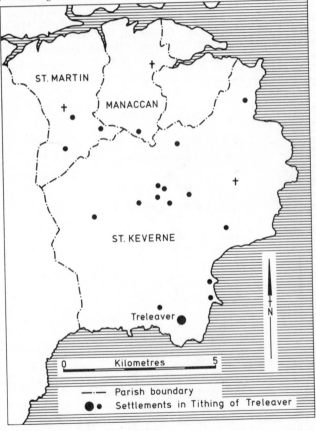

the civil duties laid on the ecclesiastical parish from the Tudor period ensured that the parish gained ascendancy over the tithing, particularly where the parish covered a comparatively small and compact territory. The parish of Collingbourne Kingston, Wiltshire (figure 7), for example, contained four tithings, the boundaries of which are known from landholding records as each was a separate estate. They lost their administrative functions, however, and it is the parish as a whole which survived as a modern civil parish (Bonney, 1969). Territorial tithings also existed in medieval Cornwall, though there they were supplanted by the parish for taxation purposes as early as the Lay Subsidy of 1327 and soon declined. Where they can be reconstructed, they sometimes cut across parish boundaries: although most of the tithing of Treleaver in the Lizard Peninsula (figure 8) lay in the parish of St Keverne, it also included holdings in four settlements in the adjacent parishes of St Martin and Manaccan (Pool, 1981).

Before leaving the question of definitions, another variant on the pattern of medieval townships must be mentioned. In some parts of England the townships which were the ancestors of the modern civil parishes were grouped in the middle ages into *villae integrae*, that is 'entire' or 'complete' vills, for the purposes of peacekeeping. Their origins are obscure but groupings of townships in this way were found in several counties in the former Danelaw in the medieval period. In the twelfth century, for example, Thedwestrey hundred in Suffolk was said to contain 24 vills which constituted 'six leets which are called *villae integrae*' (the significance of the 'leet' is discussed in chapter 8); in Rutland in 1316 the settlements of Oakham, Egleton and 'Gouthorp' were said to make one entire vill (Lees, 1926), while in Cumberland the 'five vills of Copeland', containing between them ten townships, appear to have been similar groupings. Elsewhere in Cumbria, settlements in the Lake District, which in the thirteenth century were described as vills in their own right and which descended to the present day as townships and later civil parishes, appear to have been grouped into very large 'entire vills' in the fourteenth and fifteenth centuries: the huge 'vill of Strickland Ketel', for example, embraced at least fourteen 'hamlets' (that is, later townships), including the valleys of Langdale, Kentmere and Longsleddale, and other settlements on the edge of the Lake District north of Kendal (Winchester, 1978; 1987).

Lordship and township boundaries

Township and tithing frequently, but by no means always, corresponded to an estate, often to a manor, in the middle ages. In these cases the boundaries of the administrative unit were thus those of a unit of landholding, and the influence of lordship and landownership is frequently seen in the complexities of township boundary patterns. Even where a correspondence between township and estate is not recorded, it is likely that many township boundaries reflect the fundamental and ancient division of the countryside between rural communities, providing each with not only ploughland for crops and meadows for fodder, but also pasture for livestock and sources of fuel and building materials. In short, even if lost in the mists of antiquity, the boundaries of a vill would normally have been drawn to encompass the rights in land which ensured access to the staples of life for members of a rural community.

Direct evidence of the link between landownership and the township territory is fairly frequently found in medieval documents. Where charters granting estates to new owners in the eleventh to thirteenth centuries include boundary details, the bounds they describe are often found to coincide exactly with the township boundaries shown on nineteenth-century Ordnance Survey maps. Again and again, documents recording the settlement of disputed boundaries between medieval estates confirm that estate and township boundaries were one and the same. The same was true of many tithings: in Wiltshire, for example, the factor underlying the division of a parish into tithings was frequently medieval landownership, each tithing representing a manor or smaller estate which can often be traced back to the eleventh century. Similarly, the family or institutional names which appear as suffixes to many place-names are a reminder that many townships corresponded to estates which were carved out of earlier larger units. Examples abound and two pairs of names from opposite ends of England will suffice to make the point: Yealand Conyers and Yealand Redmayne, adjacent townships in north Lancashire, preserve the names of their early thirteenth-century lords, as do the Gloucestershire vills of Duntisbourne Abbots (belonging to the abbot of St Peter's, Gloucester) and Duntisbourne Rouse (belonging to the le Rous family).

The influence of landownership on the pattern of township boundaries is particularly clearly seen in areas of late colonisation where woodland or waste taken into use by a particular estate was subsequently considered part of the same township, even where this created a multiplicity of detached portions. An extreme example of this occurred on the Essex islands of Canvey, Foulness and Wallasea. The marshes of these islands were sheep pastures intercommoned by settlements on the mainland and each island consisted of a patchwork of small detached portions of the vills with pasture rights. Canvey Island was divided between nine mainland settlements, Foulness between six and Wallasea between five. These are extreme cases of a common phenomenon, the preservation in township boundaries of ancient patterns of land use where a community had to draw on land at some distance from its core of fields to answer a particular need, often that for pasture or woodland.

Detached portions of townships can also reflect the influence of lordship at the time when empty land between settlements was being cleared and appropriated to neighbouring communities. As an example, we may take the Vale of Lorton, Cumberland (figure 9), where the townships of Lorton and Brackenthwaite met along an interlocking boundary and a detached piece of Buttermere township intruded between the other two. All three townships lay within the private forest of Derwentfells and within the bounds of the ancient parish of Brigham. The explanation of the complex boundary pattern in this small area lies in the rapid expansion of settlement in the Lake District in the thirteenth century. Lorton and Brackenthwaite, separate estates within the forest by the mid twelfth century, were probably divided by a belt of unsettled woodland or waste: Brackenthwaite was said in about 1160 to stretch south 'from the cultivated land of Lorton', a line which was presumably subject to change as colonisation took place. The interdigitated boundary between Brackenthwaite and Lorton townships and the detached pieces of Brackenthwaite in Lorton are probably the result of medieval land clearance by the two communities in a zone where rights were ill defined. Colonisation was also pushing the frontier of enclosed land up the hillside in the vicinity of Swinside. However, any new land taken in in that area was part of neither Lorton nor Brackenthwaite estates, but of the private forest belonging to the feudal overlord, the Earl of Albemarle. The tenants of the new holdings at Swinside, recorded by 1259, were thus his tenants and paid their rent to the reeve of Buttermere, the township 5 miles (8 km) away in which the Earl had tenants. That link made them members of the township community of Buttermere and their farms were thus considered to be a detached portion of the township (see Winchester, 1987).

The complexities of territorial boundaries in such areas of late colonisation are particularly amenable to study because of the comparative wealth of detailed documentation for lordship and landownership in the twelfth and thirteenth centuries. This enables us to look in some detail at the relationship between township boundaries and rights in land in areas where those rights were in the process of being claimed and settled. In many other areas, as we have seen, a township or tithing possessed some identity as a manor or lesser estate at some point between the eleventh and thirteenth centuries. Although exceptions

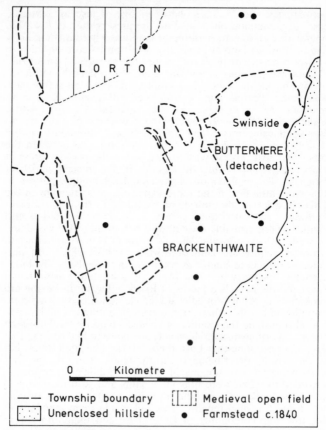

Figure 9. Township boundaries in the Vale of Lorton, Cumberland (NY 12).

could probably be quoted from almost every English county, it would seem to be a reasonable working hypothesis to suggest that the boundaries of the medieval vill (and thus, in many cases, the modern civil parish) were ultimately determined by the pattern of landholding. The next question, which is explored in chapter 5, is to look in greater detail at the question of chronology: when did the boundary lines marked on the modern map come to be fixed?

Boroughs and cities

So far we have been looking at the administrative landscape of the countryside but, in addition to the townships and tithings of rural society, medieval administrators recognised boroughs and cities as distinct and different communities. In constitutional and legal terms boroughs and cities have been described as 'islands in the sea of rural feudalism' and their separate nature is reflected in their territorial boundaries as well. The freedom of burgage tenure and the mercantile privileges of the borough community required a clear boundary to be drawn between it and the outside rural world. In practice that boundary often took the form of a physical barrier, punctuated by controllable entries, the town wall. Where an ecclesiastical parish straddled the town boundary it was often effectively bisected for purposes of civil administration and modern civil parish names sometimes record the division in the suffixes *intra* ('within') and *extra* ('without', that is outside), as in Strood Extra and Strood Intra (Kent) and St Cuthbert's Within and St Cuthbert's Without (York).

Many smaller boroughs were never walled and in such cases there was not an obvious physical feature to be taken as the community's boundary. Many settlements which were granted borough status in the twelfth and thirteenth centuries had grown 'organically' from an existing rural settlement, and the expanding urban community retained the boundaries of its forefathers. In contrast, other boroughs and market towns were 'planted', sometimes on virgin sites, and their boundaries may show that the new settlement had been carved out of the territory of another community. Ormskirk (Lancashire), for example, consisted of a township territory of only 572 acres (231 ha), carved from the corner of Burscough and Lathom townships.

Urban growth since the mid nineteenth century has resulted in almost all old towns bursting out of the confines of their medieval territory and new towns developing out of former rural settlements. The constitutions of 178 of the larger towns were put on a common footing by the Municipal Corporations Act of 1835 and their boundaries (often newly determined to reflect contemporary needs) were established by the Boundary Commission in 1837. Since then municipal boundaries have been repeatedly revised as towns have grown, swallowing up neighbouring rural townships. The spread of Derby, to take a single example, was not unusual: from an area of 1796 acres (727 ha) before 1877, successive boundary changes enlarged the borough to 8133 acres (3291 ha) by 1934.

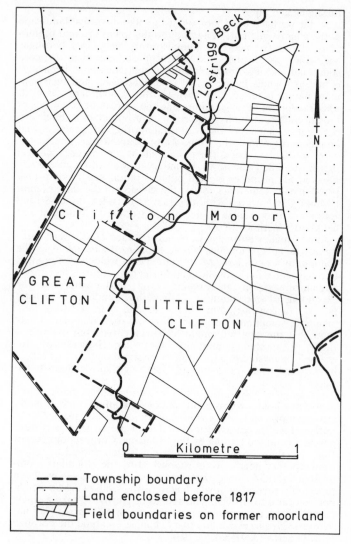

Figure 10. Clifton Moor, Cumberland (NY 02): a township boundary determined at enclosure in 1817.

5. How old are township boundaries?

In the examples given in the previous chapter, we have seen the influence of the pattern of lordship in the twelfth and thirteenth centuries on the formation of township boundaries in areas which were settled at a comparatively *late* date. By contrast, the landscape of many large swathes of the country was already old by the Norman period and, we may assume, contained long stretches of established boundaries well before that time. The main aim of this chapter is to explore the question of how old were the township boundaries in areas which were already settled by the Norman Conquest. However, parts of the boundary network, at least, came to be defined comparatively recently and we begin in the much more recent past with some of the changes which affected the boundary pattern in the nineteenth century.

The parcelling of the land surface between neighbouring communities is not complete, even today. Modern Ordnance Survey maps remind us that parts of the upland moors of northern England, like Hamsterley Common (County Durham) and Fylingdales Moor (Yorkshire North Riding), remain as land common to two or more civil parishes. These are the last vestiges of land shared by townships and thus outside the framework of township boundaries, but it should be remembered that there were many thousands of acres of such land, particularly in upland areas, before parliamentary enclosure of the commons in the late eighteenth and nineteenth centuries. The General Inclosure Acts of 1801 and 1845 empowered enclosure commissioners to determine the boundaries of any manor or parish in which land was to be enclosed. In practice this resulted in the disentangling of rights of intercommon on numerous commons. The result was that a common previously shared by two or more township communities was divided between them, generally along the artificially straight lines of the new allotments laid out in the commissioners' drawing office. A striking example of such an artificial boundary line, darting across the landscape in a series of right-angled turns, resulted from the enclosure in 1817 of Clifton Moor, near Workington (Cumberland) (figure 10), which had formerly been intercommoned by the villages of Great and Little Clifton and thus lay undivided between the two townships. As often happened, exchanges of land occurred and the field boundaries which were built did not always follow the commissioners' lines. Only a few decades after enclosure, parts of the remarkably artificial township boundary which the commissioners had laid out across Clifton Moor had been deserted by hedge and fence lines to be left as a series of unmarked straight lines cutting across the new fields. As we saw in the case of Somerton parish (figure 4), such enclosure could result in the creation of detached pieces of a parish or township to replace a common right formerly exercised on distant pastures.

The tidying up of the boundary pattern continued through the nineteenth century. Under the Tithe Commutation Act of 1836 the tithe commissioners were required to determine disputed or ill defined boundaries, and a major tidying took place in 1883 as a result of the Divided Parishes Act of 1882, whereby the thousands of detached portions, some so carefully created or confirmed only decades before, were swept away and deemed to be included in the parish by whose land they were surrounded. It is important to be aware of these nineteenth-century changes and to remember that parts of many a parish's boundaries may be of comparatively recent origin in their mapped form.

Before the formalisation of parish and township boundaries by official action (and their mapping by the Ordnance Survey) in the nineteenth century doubtful sections of boundary were liable to dispute and sporadic attempts were sometimes made to determine disputed sections. Examples of such disputes in the later middle ages and the sixteenth to eighteenth centuries are given in chapter 6. But, though numerous and generating a considerable body of documentation, they concerned only a small proportion of the many thousands of miles of township boundaries in England. If we accept that much of the remainder of the boundary network has been inherited from the middle ages, how much further back in time can we trace it? Were the boundaries of modern civil parishes laid down before the Norman Conquest and, if so, how long before? These are difficult questions which have received a good deal of attention since the 1960s. No conclusive answer can be given but this is probably mainly because no single answer will be true of the whole of England and because the evidence which must be relied on is so scant and liable to differing interpretations.

There is growing agreement that many township boundaries are a legacy from the later centuries of the Anglo-Saxon period, at the latest. Although some elements of the boundary pattern are clearly the result of post-Conquest change (whether as a result of the influence of lordship in the period of medieval colonisation, or of enclosure in the eighteenth and nineteenth centuries), many stretches of boundary were almost certainly ancient by the twelfth century. The firmest evidence for this comes from Anglo-Saxon charters, mainly of tenth-century and eleventh-century date and restricted almost entirely to the Midlands and the south, which include detailed perambulations of the estate being granted. Where these can be related to the ground, the Saxon boundary is frequently found either to correspond to that of a modern parish or township, or to describe a section of a modern unit, including part of its outer boundary. To pick a handful of examples at random, the boundaries of Ditcheat and Rimpton (Somerset) were in existence by AD 842 and the mid tenth century respectively (Aston, 1988; Costen, 1985); those of Uffington (Berkshire) by 953 (Gelling, 1978); those of Upton-on-Severn (Worcestershire) by 962 (Hooke, 1985); while a mid tenth-century charter of an estate at 'Colingburne' (Wiltshire) appears to describe the later bounds of Aughton, one of the constituent tithings of Collingbourne Kingston parish (see figure 7) (Bonney, 1969). Furthermore, it is clear from the wording of many such charters that the boundaries they describe were not being laid out anew but were already established features in the landscape, as references to the bounds of neighbouring settlements, sometimes marked by *gemære hagan* ('boundary hedges'), or to the meeting point of three or four boundaries demonstrate. Indeed, in many parts of the Midlands and the south, the appropriation of land by neighbouring communities appears to have been complete and a network of interlocking territorial boundaries established by the tenth century.

How old such boundaries were in, say, the tenth century is more difficult to determine. Much of the work on territorial patterns in the Saxon period has sought to explore the possibility that the boundaries were such stable features of the landscape that they pre-date the Anglo-Saxon settlement and are a legacy from the Romano-British period. The approach to the question which has been adopted most frequently has been to examine the relationship between recorded parish and township boundaries and known archaeological features from earlier periods. One of the pioneers of this technique in recent times has been Desmond Bonney (Bonney, 1972; 1976), who has suggested that some territorial boundaries in Wessex may have been established by the late iron age. Late Saxon charters from the region confirm that many of the boundaries recorded on nineteenth-century maps preserve the outlines of late Saxon estates. Bonney approached the question of their antiquity on several fronts. He noted that a strikingly high proportion of pagan Saxon burials of fifth-century or sixth-century date lie on or very close to parish boundaries and suggested that this indicated that burials were deliberately placed on what were then accepted boundaries, thus taking the antiquity of the boundary network back to the earliest phase of Saxon settlement. But the relationship of the recorded boundary network to earlier archaeological sites led him to suggest that parts of it may have been inherited from an even more distant period. In some parts of Wiltshire, for example, Roman roads are followed for many miles by parish boundaries; in other parts, parish boundaries almost completely ignore the Roman road network. Clearly, where a parish boundary follows a Roman road, its present line must post-date the construction of the road; but is the converse true? If parish boundaries ignore such a major landscape feature as a Roman road, can we conclude that they were already established when the road was built? Bonney suggested that we can in Wiltshire. He noted that there was a relationship between the distribution of pre-Roman iron age settlements and the use or non-use of Roman roads as boundaries: the roads tended not to be used as boundaries where iron age settlements were densest, but they were used where there was little evidence for iron age settlement. In other words, it seems possible, at least,

Figure 11. North-west Nottinghamshire (SK 68): the relationship between township boundaries and Romano-British fields. (After Unwin, 1983.)

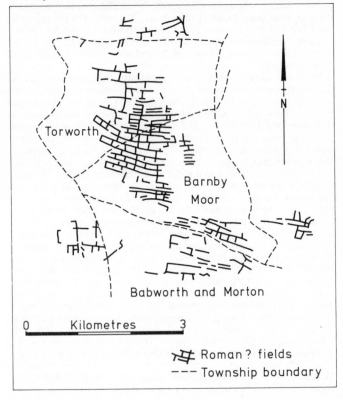

that the boundary network in the areas where Roman roads were ignored is a legacy from the iron age, whereas it post-dates the Roman period in those other parts of the county in which Roman roads are followed by boundaries.

Desmond Bonney's conclusions have not gone unchallenged and there is particular doubt about the validity of his argument that the placing of pagan Anglo-Saxon burials on boundaries is evidence that the boundaries were older than the burials (see Goodier, 1984). Even if an iron age origin is accepted for the medieval boundary network in parts of Wessex, recent work suggests that the situation was very different in other parts of England. In north-west Nottinghamshire, for example, aerial photography has revealed an extensive lost landscape of field boundaries, probably of Roman date, underlying the medieval countryside. When the network of medieval township boundaries is superimposed on the Roman landscape the two are found to bear hardly any relationship to each other (figure 11), strongly suggesting a definite discontinuity between the Roman and medieval patterns of land occupation. In that area the township boundaries may have originated in the Anglo-Saxon period but they cannot be pushed back beyond the dark ages (Unwin, 1983). A similar conclusion has been drawn from more tenuous evidence in south Norfolk. Here, in contrast to the east Midlands, there are hints that much of the nineteenth-century field pattern of small rectangular fields has been inherited from the Celtic period: even Roman roads appear as intrusions, cutting through the farming landscape. The medieval parish boundaries appear likewise to have been imposed on an existing landscape: in contrast to Nottinghamshire, for much of their course they follow the hedgebanks of the ancient rectangular field pattern, but they make use of minor as well as major lines in the field pattern and they also follow later intrusive features such as footpaths and lanes which cut across the grain of the countryside (Williamson, 1986).

In trying to ascertain the antiquity of the pattern created by the boundaries of medieval vills we are peering 'through a glass darkly'. The Nottinghamshire evidence against continuity from the Romano-British period is perhaps the firmest, but the evidence mustered by Bonney and others in favour of continuity raises tantalising possibilities that, in some parts of England at least, long sections of the parish and township boundary network recorded on nineteenth-century maps may have a time-depth of almost two thousand years. The explanation of these apparently contradictory conclusions is probably to be found in the different experiences of different parts of the country in the late Anglo-Saxon and Norman periods. If we accept that much of the boundary network of Wessex was ancient by the tenth century, there are good grounds for assuming that the boundary patterns of the Danelaw or the northern counties, for example, are likely to be much younger. The disruption of the Danish conquest of eastern England in the later ninth century, the struggle for political control in the Danelaw in the early tenth, the continuing political instability of northern England in the early eleventh century, and William the Conqueror's punitive 'harrying of the north' in 1069 and 1070 must have caused repeated disruption to the rhythm of farming life in those areas. Indeed, settlement historians are now suggesting that the late Anglo-Saxon period and the decades immediately after the Conquest were a crucial era in the development of village settlement in England, with the rural population being concentrated in larger villages, some of which, particularly in the north, show evidence of deliberate planning by landowners (see Roberts, 1987; Taylor, 1983). In such a context of deliberate change it is possible that the territorial framework of the countryside was rewritten and that the very regular patterns of parish boundaries seen in areas such as Lincoln Edge (figure 14) or the Vale of Pickering may be a legacy from that phase of settlement history.

6. Boundaries and boundary markers

Surveys and perambulations

The Ordnance Survey map is the usual starting point for a study of local territorial boundaries. Civil parish boundaries were marked on successive editions of the One Inch (1:63,360) series and on the First Series of the 1:50,000 sheets which replaced them. They are not shown on modern 1:50,000 ('Landranger') maps but are given on the 1:25,000 ('Pathfinder') series, which is one of the local historian's most valuable tools. In order to overcome boundary changes made since the nineteenth century, anyone studying parish boundaries should refer to nineteenth-century Ordnance Survey maps, particularly the Six Inch (1:10,560) and Twenty-five Inch (1:2500) series published for each county, the first editions of which were surveyed between about 1845 and 1885, and the earlier one inch to one mile sheets, known as the 'Tithe Index' series because they were overprinted with the names and boundaries of each unit for which a separate tithe commutation award was made. The nineteenth-century Ordnance Survey Six Inch and Twenty-five Inch maps describe local administrative boundaries in great detail; indeed, the surveyors were charged with producing definitive maps, being required under the Ordnance Survey Act of 1841 to ascertain and map all public boundaries, drawing on local knowledge where boundaries had not been mapped before. The resulting maps delineated the whole spectrum of local administrative units functioning in the nineteenth century: counties, hundreds and wapentakes; boroughs and cities and their wards; parishes, townships and even 'divisions of townships'. Each boundary was marked on the map as a dotted or pecked line, each section annotated to specify the exact line it followed, using abbreviations as in the following table:

Key to boundary descriptions on Ordnance Survey Six Inch Maps
1. Following watercourses
   - C.S.   centre of stream
   - S.S.   side of stream
   - S.D.   side of drain
2. Following roads
   - C.R.   centre of road
3. Following field boundaries
   - S.F.   side of fence
   - F.C.   face of cop (i.e. hedgebank)
   - R.H.   root of hedge
   - F.W.   face of wall
   - C.F.   centre of fence
   - T.C.   top of cop

        C.W.   centre of wall
4. Across open land
        Def.   defaced
        T.S.   track of stream
        Und.   undefined

The published maps were the end result of a detailed process of local enquiry and the original records of the surveyors can yield useful additional information, particularly the 'Boundary Remark Books' for each parish, which contain notes on the process of ascertaining the boundary and annotated sketch maps of boundary details (Aldsworth, 1982).

The Ordnance Surveyors thus pinned down boundaries which had in many cases never been mapped before, and they provided the base from which we must work today. It is important to remember that the lines they mapped were those in current use at the time of the survey and thus incorporated recent modifications and rationalisation as well as ancient features. The work of the Ordnance Survey also led to the mapping of many thousands of place-names, some of which may yield evidence of the existence of boundaries. By far the commonest of these are stream names such as Merebrook and Merebeck, derived from the Old English *maere*, 'a boundary', but there are several other words which preserve the memory of early boundaries and these are listed in the appendix.

Before the mapping of the Six Inch Ordnance Survey sheets, boundaries were passed down by word of mouth and by ritual 'beating of the bounds', and disputes between neighbouring communities over the exact line of a boundary were frequent. The 'beating of the bounds' was an age-old ritual carried out in Rogation Week, the time between the fifth Sunday after Easter and Ascension Day. In this early summer custom local officials (the parson, if the bounds to be beaten were those of the parish; the constable of a township; the steward of the court of a manor) accompanied by a throng of inhabitants, young and old, perambulated the boundary (see plate 9). This communal occasion was often accompanied by liberal quantities of food and drink but it served a serious purpose, namely to keep fresh in the local memory boundaries which may never have been written down or plotted on a map. To serve that end, there arose the time-honoured custom of giving the young lads in the procession a memorable (usually unpleasant) experience at particular points along the boundary as an aid to memory. Examples of these rough rustic rituals are recorded across England in depositions made by witnesses during lawsuits over disputed boundaries; two will suffice here to give a flavour of the occasion.

The first comes from Exmoor (Somerset), where the boundaries were in dispute in 1678. William Gregory, an elderly farmer from Exford, remembered how, at the age of seven in 1606, he went on the perambulation of Exford parish. As they passed one of the boundary stones, one of the older inhabitants called to William to 'put his finger on a meerestone, saying it was soe hot it would scald him', which he did. The man then 'immediately thereupon layd hold on [William's] hand and did wring one of his fingers sorely that for the present it grieved him very much, and said, "Remember that this is a boundstone and is a boundary to the parish of Exford"' (MacDermot, 1973). If this seems harsh treatment for a small boy, compare it with the outright violence meted out by the inhabitants of Ormskirk (Lancashire). Robert Fidler, a 47-year-old tallow chandler giving evidence about the boundaries of Ormskirk in 1635, recalled how as a boy he 'had his eares pulled and was set on his head upon a mearestone neere to a newe ditch on Ormiskirke Moore and had his head knocked to the said stone to the end to make him the better to remember that the same stone was a boundary stone' (Lancashire Record Office, DDK/1601/3).

Today most people are only vaguely aware of the boundary of their local community and it is easy to forget how vitally important the knowledge of boundaries could be before the nineteenth century. Not only did they establish the individual's relationship with a parish church and with the civil local government system, but they also defined common rights and thus had a direct economic significance. That also applied to the increasingly contentious issue of tithes when, in many parishes, the right to take tithes became a saleable commodity after the Dissolution of the Monasteries. The right to take tithe was bought and sold, leased and sublet and the position of a parish or township boundary determined the value of the right: if a boundary was in dispute, the extent and value of the tithes was in question. As an example of the reality of parish boundaries in the lives of our ancestors we may take a dispute about the boundary between the townships of Astley and Bedford, near Leigh (Lancashire) about 1590. The tithes of Astley and Bedford had been sold to different people and the two tithe collectors clashed when attempting to collect tithes in an area where the boundary was in dispute, and where a new house had been built close to, if not straddling, the boundary. The Astley tithe collector claimed a tithe goose from George Hindley, the owner of the house in question, because the eggs had hatched in the new house, which, he claimed, was wholly in Astley. The Bedford collector also claimed the goose and they referred the matter to George Hindley. He 'did award the said goose to belonge to Mr Urmston [the owner of Bedford tithes] by reason that the gooselinges weare as hee said hatched under the higher end of a benche then in the newe howse, saying that soe much under the same benche as a goose could sit on was in [Bedford]'. But the witness 'thinketh hee had wronge that he had not the goose, for he thinketh all the newe howse is in Astley'! (Lancashire Record Office, DDHm).

Boundary disputes and their resolution

As we saw in the previous chapter, the network of parish and township boundaries mapped in the nineteenth century had been at least a thousand years in the making, the final stages taking place only in the nineteenth century itself. Looking back at the process of boundary definition over the millennium or more, we can think of it as reflecting the gradually closer definition of rights as land came to be appropriated by individuals. The empty spaces between rural communities disappeared so that the territory of one abutted on that of its neighbours and a fixed boundary was born. In the process it was inevitable that disputes would occur where one community felt it had rights in land claimed by a neighbour. From the earliest period title deeds, the records of the Courts of Equity and the proceedings of manor courts all contain evidence of disputed boundaries and we may be certain that these form only the tip of the iceberg.

Some disputes appear to have been so long-lasting that reference to a disputed area was made permanent in the form of a place-name. The Old English element *threap*, fairly common in minor place-names, records long-forgotten boundary disputes. Many of the places bearing such names as Threapland, Threapwood or Threapmuir were probably fairly small disputed areas but two represented larger blocks of land. Threapwood, on the Anglo-Welsh border near Wrexham, was a tract of woodland between Cheshire and Flintshire, reputed to be part of no county, parish or township, paying no land tax or rates, and beyond the jurisdiction of justices of the peace in either county. It was a genuine 'no man's land', disputed and thereby never brought into the administrative structure. The second was the Debateable Land on the western marches of England and Scotland, between the rivers Esk and Sark, which was formerly known as 'Threpelands'. The Anglo-Scottish border was finally fixed only in 1552 when these 'Threpelands' were divided between the two nations and the line made permanent by the construction of the Scots Dyke (plate 10). Other place-name elements recording boundary disputes include *calenge*, 'a challenge or dispute', found again in connection with disputed woodland as in Callingwood (Staffordshire) and Callans Wood (Worcestershire); *ceast*, 'strife, contention', found in Chesland (Wiltshire) and Chest Wood (Essex), both of which lie close to parish boundaries; and *flit*, a term with a similar meaning occurring in Flitnell (Northamptonshire) and Flitteridge (Sussex), meaning 'the disputed hill' and 'ridge' respectively.

Disputes were obviously most likely to occur across land beyond the limits of a community's enclosed farmland and, again and again, place-names and historical records from the Norman Conquest through to the eighteenth century throw up evidence of boundary disputes over ancient woodland, open moorland and fen or marsh. The survey of Cheshire place-names noted two further Threapwoods and three Theaphursts as minor names, recording disputed woodland along township boundaries. The Lincolnshire folios of Domesday Book record disputed woodland and the interdigitation of parishes along tortuous boundaries through ancient woodland seen there (figure 12) and in many other areas almost certainly bears silent witness to the sorting out of conflicting claims in a valuable resource as the medieval population grew.

Numerous disputes over open waste, whether moorland or wetland, are recorded in legal papers during the sixteenth and seventeenth centuries, some rumbling on from generation to generation. Behind many such disputes lurked pressures to extend the limits of improved farmland by enclosure or drainage, thus threatening the *status quo* whereby waste had, in practice, been intercommoned by the inhabitants of settlements around its periphery. It is easy to see how action by one community could tip the delicate balance of shared use and cause grievance: a valuable pasture right or right to cut peat for fuel was under threat. A handful of examples from a range of very different landscapes will suffice to illustrate the process.

In Shropshire, for example, the Wealdmoors, an area of wetland stretching north of Wellington, were the subject of a series of lawsuits between about 1565 and 1650 as attempts to drain and enclose pieces of land from it forced the issue of the manorial, and thus the township, boundaries within it. Further south the parish boundaries across the hill grazings of the Long Mynd also continued to be challenged until comparatively recently, disputes bubbling over into lawsuits in 1698 (over the boundary between Ratlinghope and Church Stretton) and 1743 (concerning the boundary between Woolstaston and Stretton) (Shropshire Record Office, 93/25; Shropshire Library Local Studies Department, Deed 6583).

On the Fylde coast in Lancashire disputes over the division of Layton Hawes, the sandy wastes fringing the sea between the modern resorts of Blackpool and Lytham St Annes, broke out repeatedly in the sixteenth and seventeenth centuries. In 1272 a boundary line across the Hawes, marked by two crosses, had been fixed, separating that part belonging to Layton in the north from that part belonging to Kelgrimoles (a settlement near Lytham later washed away by the sea). Disputes between the

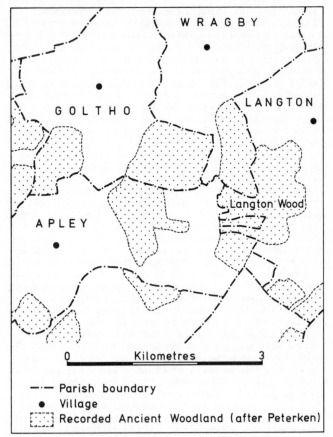

Figure 12. Parish boundaries and ancient woodland in central Lincoln-shire (TF 17). The extent of recorded woodland is from Peterken, 1981.

lords of Layton and Lytham about rights in the Hawes are recorded in 1338 and 1509 and an acrimonious quarrel over the boundary came to a head and was brought before the Duchy Court of Lancaster in 1530 and again in 1532. The monks of Lytham Priory, who were lords of the manor of Lytham, seem to have attempted to fence off part of the waste, an 'improvement' which was met by direct action by the inhabitants of Layton, who gathered on the debated land, pulled down four hundred 'rodds' of fencing, drove away the priory's cattle and pulled down one of the old timber boundary crosses. The court decreed twice that the ancient boundary should be respected but the dispute flared up again in 1608. The location of the drowned settlement of Kelgrimoles, intercommoning, and differences of opinion over the identification of a cross in the Hawes combined to give the dispute considerable potential across the decades (Fishwick, 1896).

As we have seen, a final tidying up of remaining undefined or doubtful boundaries took place in the early nineteenth century. As well as the activities of enclosure commissioners, the Tithe Commutation Act of 1836 empowered the Tithe Commissioners to determine parish and township boundaries and to produce definitive boundary awards. Over 180 such formal clarifications were made by the Commissioners and are now preserved in the Public Record Office (class TITH/1). Some, such as that fixing the boundary of Winton township (Westmorland) by placing a series of boundary stones across the wild fell country south of Stainmore, settled boundaries over open rough grazing land; others, such as that defining ten outliers of Christian Malford parish (Wiltshire) scattered in the parish of Bremhill, made certain the boundaries of detached portions.

Boundary stones and boundary markers

As we have seen, the boundaries of parish and township were kept fresh in the communal memory by the Rogation Week custom of beating the bounds. As long as a boundary kept to the line of a stream, a road or a field boundary, the procession could be guided by the feature they were following; the excitement began when the boundary left the security of such features and struck out across open land or through woodland. During their perambulation the inhabitants would sometimes leave a series of marks on features along their route to reinforce their claim to the boundary. At Croydon (Surrey), for example, in the sixteenth century the parishioners 'sett their crosse to the side of' the Vicar's Oak, a great oak tree on Penge Common claimed by them to be the boundary between Croydon and Battersea parishes (Public Record Office, E134/20 Eliz/E.7). At Ratlinghope (Shropshire) when the parson and churchwardens perambulated the parish boundary in the seventeenth century they 'in severall places cutt markes, to witt the first letters of the lord of the mannor's name . . . , in the outermost parts of the bounds of the said parish' (Shropshire Record Office, 93/25). As late as the nineteenth century the Ordnance Survey maps show boundaries in Epping Forest (Essex) defined by boundary marks on pollarded trees through the woodland.

Such marks were more or less ephemeral in character and it is not surprising to find evidence from an early date of stones and crosses being deliberately erected to mark a boundary line. Anglo-Saxon charters from the west Midlands show that crucifixes, sometimes fixed to oak trees, had been set up on the boundaries of church estates by the tenth century and there are also references to *mærstanæ* ('boundary stones'). Both appear usually to have been placed where a boundary crossed a road or path (Hooke, 1981). By the fifteenth century the moorland boundary between the monastic estate of St Bees township and neighbouring Egremont township (Cumberland) had been marked by 'great stones' placed on the waste leading to a series of stone crosses, at least one of which was carved with the 'sign' of St Bees. Boundaries which were finally fixed by formal decree were also sometimes marked by deliberately erected stones. In 1605, for example, when the county boundary between Lancashire and Yorkshire between Colne and Ickornshaw was settled by a Duchy of Lancaster commission, five stones were placed along a 2 mile stretch and each was given a name: 'Kingstone' and 'Erlestone' were probably so named in honour of the lords of the two manors; while 'Sir Steven's stone', 'Sergeante's stone' and 'Attorney's stone' record the identity of three of the commissioners who laid out the boundary: Sir Steven Tempest; Richard Hutton, serjeant-at-law; and Thomas Tyldesley, the King's attorney in Lancashire (Public Record Office, DL44/678). Similarly, the perambulation of Waltham Forest (Essex) by parliamentary commissioners in 1642 led to the erection of inscribed and dated stones along the boundary.

The boundary stones marked by the initials 'BS' on Ordnance Survey maps take many forms. Some are humble pillars, devoid of any inscription; others carry the names or initials of the parishes which meet at that point (see plates 1-5). Most were either placed as sight lines to define a boundary across open waste, or, perhaps most commonly, mark the point where a boundary crosses a road. Roadside boundary stones are a reminder of the parochial basis of highway maintenance before the reorganisation of local government in the late nineteenth century. The Highways Act of 1555 placed responsibility for road maintenance with the parish, though in northern counties the township usually took on the responsibility, as did the tithing in parts of the south. The limits of a parish, township or tithing along its public roads thus became a matter of practical importance and boundary stones came to be erected. Most are of no great antiquity, many being the result of nineteenth-century legislation. The Highway Act of 1835, for example, empowered local justices to order stones or posts to be set up where, as a result of the Act, a boundary which had run down the centre of a road was modified to give each parish total responsibility for half the length of the road they had formerly held in common. The Poor Law Amendment Act of 1844 encouraged the erection of boundary stones more generally by allowing the costs of setting them up and maintaining them to be defrayed by the local Poor Rate.

Such stones and posts, whether medieval or modern, were deliberately placed along a boundary to give tangible substance to it. But many boundaries included in their circuits landscape features which had been chosen, because of their distinctive nature, as the point to which a territorial unit reached, particularly over open ground. Across the medieval countryside there appear to have been numerous 'hoarstones', natural boundary stones which were distinctively hoary, probably through being covered by a growth of lichen. The term, derived from the Old English *har* ('hoary, grey'), has found its way on to the modern map in minor place-names such as Harston (Leicestershire, near the county boundary with Lincolnshire) and Hoarstone (Worcestershire). The 'Hoar Stone' on the boundary of Enstone parish in Oxfordshire was a neolithic burial chamber which 'stood like a beacon on the hills' and was not only used as a boundary marker by the Anglo-Saxons but also gave its name (as 'Enna's stone') to the parish. In the north of England the 'great, grey stones' referred to in some medieval charter bounds were similar features and have also come down to us in place-names, such as Greystone (Yorkshire North Riding) and Greystoneley (Lancashire). Such names are a memory of an ancient practice, the choosing of a distinctive boulder as a boundary marker which then became a permanent feature in a changing landscape, gathering moss and lichen and becoming distinctively hoary and grey.

On otherwise featureless moorland in the north of England large glacial erratics were sometimes used as boundary markers, such as the 'Great Stone of Fourstones' on the Lancashire-Yorkshire boundary between Tatham and Bentham parishes, a huge block of millstone grit, originally perhaps one of four such stones on the moorland boundary. A similar example is Navelin Stone on the boundary between Cleator and Brisco townships in Cumberland (see plates 6-7). The boulder is named as 'Avellan stane' in the boundary clause of a charter of about 1210, along with another stone, now lost, called 'Stainbrennan'. Both had been given the names of individuals — Avenel and Brendan (probably men living no later than the twelfth century) — a practice also found in Anglo-Saxon charter boundaries in the west Midlands. Across such open country it was not only stones which were chosen to mark a boundary line. Exmoor Forest, for example, was defined by a combination of crosses, boundary stones, cairns and a tree (see plate 8), Dartmoor Forest by a series of stone heaps or 'boroughs'.

Even today, despite hedgerow clearance, road widening and the other assaults of the twentieth century, the countryside contains a rich but largely forgotten legacy of boundary markers, ancient and modern, in many cases marking points where the feet of countless generations of countrymen had trudged along the limits of their lands during Rogation Week.

Figure 13. Analysis of township boundaries in the Eden valley, Westmorland: 10 km grid square NY 62.

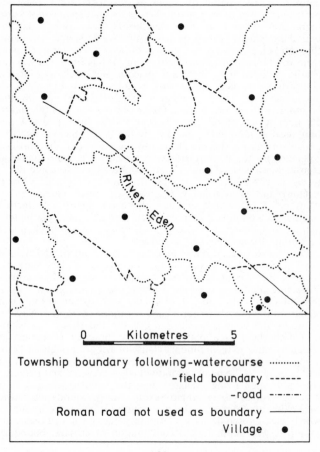

7. Analysing the boundary pattern

This chapter returns to the pattern created by the network of boundaries recorded on the large-scale Ordnance Survey map and explores some of the questions which are raised by studying that pattern in a local area. It is concerned more with questions than answers as our picture of how the administrative landscape evolved at a local level is still very incomplete. We do not know, for example, how much of the boundary pattern is the result of slow evolution across the centuries as the enclosure of new land extinguished woodland and waste and led to hard and fast boundaries being agreed by neighbouring settlements, and how much was imposed from above by higher authority on an already settled landscape. There is still great scope for painstaking local research to try to explain the complexities of the boundary patterns found in the English countryside and this chapter suggests various directions a detailed analysis of local boundary patterns might take.

One approach involves a simple classification of the boundaries shown on the modern map. This enables the boundary network of different parts of England to be compared and can show up graphically the regional diversity of boundary patterns. A simple first step involves a fairly straightforward two-fold classification. Sections of boundary may be assigned first of all to one of two categories: those following *natural features* and those following *man-made features*. Natural features consist largely of rivers and streams, or the route of a former watercourse, and watersheds along the crests of hills. Man-made features include roads and tracks, field boundaries of all sorts and clearly artificial lines across open land. Secondly, boundaries following man-made features may be further classified by placing them on a 'scale of interdigitation', ranging from a straight or smoothly curving line at one extreme to a zigzag pattern, where the boundary makes frequent changes of direction, at the other. Except where it follows a pre-existing straight feature (a Roman road is the obvious example), we may postulate that a dominant straight or almost straight boundary line is a planned feature, deliberately placed across the landscape, whereas a boundary which twists and turns will presumably do so because it is respecting existing features of the human landscape such as field boundaries.

Such a simple classification can raise some interesting questions. Compare, for example, the pattern of township boundaries in two 10 km squares, one in the Eden valley north of Appleby in Cumbria (NY 62) (figure 13), the other along Lincoln Edge, south of Lincoln (SK 95) (figure 14). The territories described by the boundaries in each area are markedly

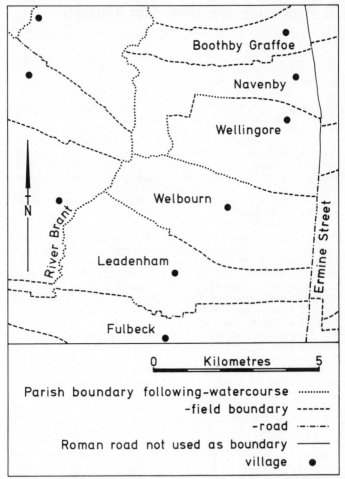

Figure 14. Analysis of parish boundaries on Lincoln Edge: 10 km grid square SK 95.

different: those in the Eden valley can best be described as 'irregular' in shape, with many of the boundaries following streams, while those in Lincolnshire take the form of fairly regular strips, defined largely by field boundaries running back from the river Brant. How do we begin to explain these

46

differences? To see them simply as the result of the contrast between the broken drumlin topography of the Eden valley and the linear scarp and vale topography of Lincoln Edge does not provide an answer. Parish boundaries are not 'natural' features and do not draw themselves. We have, rather, to begin to think in terms of piecemeal 'organic' evolution for the pattern in the Eden valley in contrast to a pattern in Lincolnshire which it is hard to see developing without a degree of imposed planning. One of the man-made lines followed by the Lincolnshire boundaries is Ermine Street, the Roman road along the High Dyke. In the southern part of the map extract it forms the eastern boundary of Fulbeck, Leadenham and Welbourn parishes, giving each a section of heathland between it and the scarp under which the villages lie. To the north, where Ermine Street runs closer to the scarp, the boundaries of Wellingore, Navenby and Boothby Graffoe almost ignore the road and are drawn to give each a share of heathland east of the road. The principal determinant of the boundaries along this section of the High Dyke was probably not so much the presence of the Roman road as a 'natural' boundary, but rather the need to allot each community a sufficiently large share of heathland grazing. Similarly, as the scarp-foot settlements swung away from Ermine Street and towards the river in the south of the extract, even the river Brant was forsaken with Leadenham and Fulbeck both including land on its further side. In terms of the 'degree of interdigitation' exhibited by these Lincolnshire boundaries, we may say that in general they follow remarkably smooth straight lines. Are these 'primary' boundaries, laid out to provide a framework to the patterns of land use which developed around each village? If so, how do we account for the occasional sudden steps along the boundaries, which suggest that the boundary has been dictated by a pre-existing feature in the field pattern? These are some of the questions which surface when we start to examine the boundary pattern in a locality.

Some distinctive boundary patterns

Another approach is to pick out distinctive elements in the boundary pattern and to ask whether any conclusions can be drawn about the processes which give rise to particular features. One such element has already been discussed in chapters 3 and 4, namely the phenomenon of the *detached portion*, where an outlying piece of one parish or township lay as an island surrounded by land belonging to another administrative territory. The conclusion in each case was that such detached portions preserved the memory of early rights in land (whether outlying parts of an estate, pasture rights on waste at a distance from the main area of settlement, or rights to tithes from land shared with another parish), even if the actual boundaries of the detached portions were determined only at a fairly late date. The following paragraphs highlight half a dozen other distinctive features in the boundary pattern and suggest ways in which they might have come into being.

Artificially straight lines (figure 15). A boundary that runs as straight as a ruler must clearly be the result of a deliberate decision to ignore topographical features. The choice of a Roman road as a boundary line, as at Denton (County Durham, figure 15), is perhaps the explanation which springs most readily to mind but by no means all straight sections of boundary can be explained in this way. Many (perhaps most) represent the latest generation of boundary making in the division of commons between communities at parliamentary enclosure in the late eighteenth and early nineteenth centuries: as we have seen (figure 10), the boundaries of new fields laid out on the former common were used as township boundaries in such cases. Indeed, Roman roads apart, the ability to drive a dead straight fence, hedge or wall line across the countryside implies the use of comparatively modern surveying techniques. However, some straight edges originated not as fence lines but as boundaries running directly across open land between two fixed points which had sometimes been fixed at a comparatively early date and in turn determined the position of a future fence line. The artificially straight sections in the boundary of Thistleton (Lancashire, figure 15), appear to be such a case. The straight southern boundary had certainly been defined by 1595 and they probably represent the division of sections of moorland, moss and wet carr between neighbouring communities in the medieval period. When these wastes were enclosed, in the sixteenth or early seventeenth centuries, the earlier division lines were respected and fossilised in the field pattern.

Interlocking boundaries (figure 16). Cases of extreme interdigitation, where the territories of two parishes or townships interlock along a zigzag boundary, have been mentioned already. In the cases of the Brackenthwaite-Lorton boundary in Cumberland (figure 9) and the boundaries in Langton Wood, Lincolnshire (figure 12), the explanation seems to lie in the division of an area of late-surviving woodland or waste in which rights were doubtful or even disputed. Not all interlocking boundaries are to be accounted for in this way. Even Anglo-Saxon charters appear to describe a boundary pattern found frequently on modern maps in which a boundary proceeds as a series of short sections at right angles to each other, producing a ladder of steps (Hooke, 1981). Boundaries such as those illustrated in figure 16 can hardly have arisen other than by the division of existing field

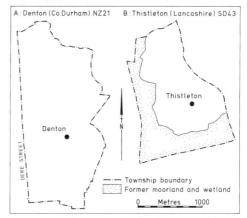

*Figure 15 (right).
Artificially straight
boundaries.*

A: Denton (Co.Durham) NZ21   B: Thistleton (Lancashire) SD43

Thistleton

Denton

DERE STREET

—··—··— Township boundary

▒▒▒ Former moorland and wetland

0   Metres   1000

*Figure 16 (below).
Interlocking
boundaries.*

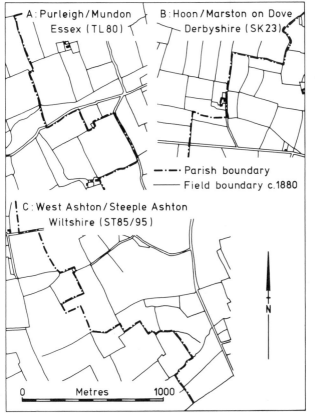

A: Purleigh/Mundon
Essex (TL80)

B: Hoon/Marston on Dove
Derbyshire (SK23)

—··—··— Parish boundary

———— Field boundary c.1880

C: West Ashton/Steeple Ashton
Wiltshire (ST85/95)

0   Metres   1000

1. Cross-marked stone, perhaps medieval in date, on the boundary between Thurstaston and Irby townships in the Wirral, Cheshire.

2. One of a numbered series of eighteenth-century stones marking the boundary of Little Caldy township, Cheshire, across open heathland.

3. Simple sandstone pillar, marked with the initials 'A' and 'C', on the boundary of Clapham and Austwick townships, Yorkshire West Riding, where it runs in a straight line across open moorland.

4. One of the distinctive roadside boundary stones in the Craven district of Yorkshire, probably of early nineteenth-century date.

5. Nineteenth-century boundary stone with an iron plate, defining the limit of Ainstable High Quarter, one of the two highway divisions of Ainstable parish, Cumberland.

6. Navelin Stone, a large boulder which has marked the boundary between the townships of Brisco and Cleator, Cumberland, since at least 1200.

7. Navelin Stone as depicted on an estate plan of 1750.

Navelin Stone

High Brisco.

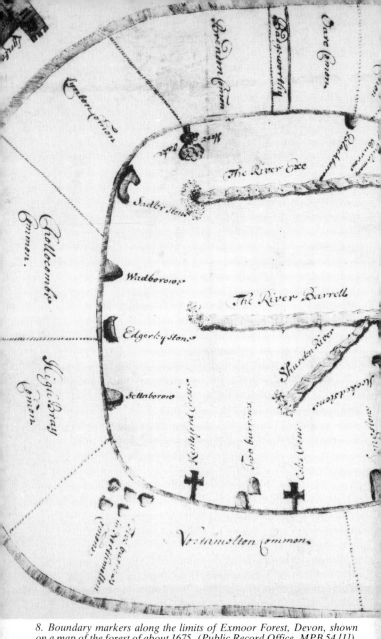

8. *Boundary markers along the limits of Exmoor Forest, Devon, shown on a map of the forest of about 1675. (Public Record Office, MPB 54 [1]).*

9. *Beating the bounds of Edgmond parish, Shropshire, about 1933.*

10. *The Scots Dyke, constructed in 1552 to divide the 'Threpelands', the disputed territory on the border between England and Scotland north-east of Gretna.*

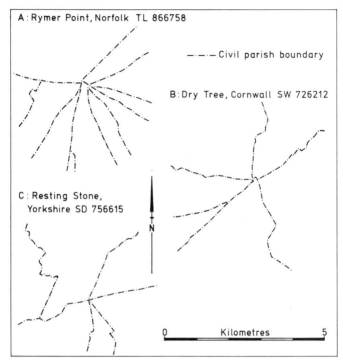

Figure 17. Converging boundaries.

patterns between two administrative territories, the line of the boundary being determined by pre-existing enclosures or headlands in an open field.

Converging boundaries (figure 17). In several different parts of England a striking pattern of territorial boundaries is found, where a number of parishes all converge on a single point. The explanation usually lies in the division of an area of rough grazing land between the communities around its edge in such a way as to allot a share to each. Three examples are shown on figure 17: in the Lizard Peninsula five parishes converge at the Dry Tree on Goonhilly Downs; in the Breckland of Norfolk eleven parishes converged on a cluster of small meres at Rymer Point; and at the Resting Stone in the Bowland fells of the West Riding of Yorkshire five townships met on a hilltop. In each case we are probably seeing a reserve of pasture originally intercommoned by the communities around its edge. When the radiating boundary patterns came to be established is not known, though it has been suggested that one of the boundaries converging on the Dry Tree on Goonhilly Downs is recorded in the bounds of Traboe, an estate in St Keverne parish, in AD 967 (Rackham, 1986).

Deviation from an obvious line (figure 18). When a boundary is examined in detail, it is not uncommon to find a short section where a well marked feature which has been followed for some distance is abruptly ignored for a while and then rejoined. Such deviations in the course of a boundary cannot have happened by chance and we must suppose that there is a reason for them, even though an explanation may not be immediately obvious. Some deviations preserve the memory of lost features in the landscape. Perhaps this is most clearly visible where a boundary follows the ancient course of a stream or river which has subsequently been straightened or has changed course by natural processes. Very common are the lines of old oxbow lakes preserved by a parish boundary long after the river has cut through the narrow neck, as in the section of the Ribble shown in figure 18B. The outline of former earthworks, whether field boundaries or archaeological sites, are often similarly preserved in a boundary line: a striking and unusual example occurs on the boundary between Butcombe and Wrington (Somerset) where the boundary makes two semicircular deviations from a hedgerow to follow the edges of lost circular prehistoric enclosures (Rackham, 1986). In other cases a deviation is the result of a recorded boundary dispute. The boundary of the township of Hardhorn-with-Newton in Lancashire (which coincided with the manor of Staining) follows for most of its southern

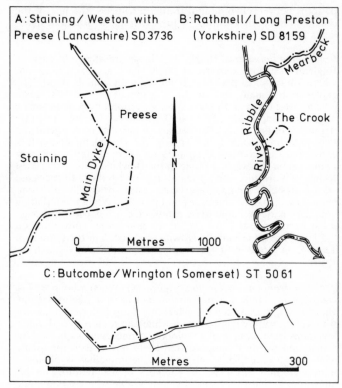

Figure 18. Boundary deviations.

and eastern course à drainage ditch cut through the centre of former wet carr land which lay between the farmland of Staining and adjacent communities. In the section illustrated the boundary suddenly swings away from the ditch, first to take in land beyond the watercourse, and then back to give the neighbouring community of Preese land on the Staining side of the ditch. This local aberration is almost certainly the result of a dispute over the carr in this area between the lords of Staining and Preese which came to a head in a lawsuit in 1523.

Roads as boundaries. Not only Roman roads appear as elements in the boundary network: main roads, minor roads, lanes, tracks and footpaths all coincide with parish boundaries in places. When interpreting roads as boundaries it is important first to distinguish between local roads and paths, linking a settlement to its fields or to a neighbouring settlement, and long-distance routes. The latter may be thought of in the same way as Roman roads, durable and obvious features in the landscape, which thus make good clear boundaries. An alignment of roads, tracks and

Figure 19. Parishes with 'panhandles'.

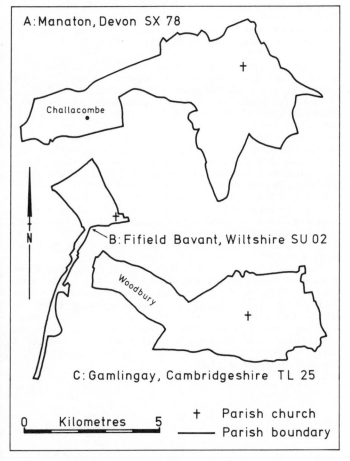

footpaths, parts of which are followed by parish boundaries, is probably evidence of such an ancient routeway. Minor local roads frequently coincide with parish boundaries in some parts of England, notably in such anciently enclosed landscapes as that of Devon. Although some may be early roads which were borrowed as boundaries, many may have evolved the other way round. Professor W. G. Hoskins has drawn attention to such lanes, suggesting that the deep and narrow lane enclosed by a massive double hedgebank which forms the boundary between the parishes of Cadbury and Stockleigh Pomeroy (Devon) probably dates back to the Anglo-Saxon period (Hoskins, 1967). In this as in other cases the line of an estate and parish boundary appears to have developed into a path or track, and some such lanes survive today as minor roads.

Parishes with 'panhandles' (figure 19). The boundaries of a parish sometimes swing out to embrace a tongue of land projecting into a neighbouring parish. There are no doubt a variety of explanations for such a pattern but the examples shown in figure 19 all appear to have a similar origin. In each case the projecting 'panhandle' had been a separate estate which had come to be placed in the parish to which it now appears to form an uncomfortable appendage. Woodbury, for example, the projecting section of Gamlingay parish, Cambridgeshire, was a separate manor from the twelfth century. The remarkable shape of Fifield Bavant parish, Wiltshire, appears to be the result of the combination of two eleventh-century estates into one manor, the long thin strip of the parish being identified with a one-hide estate in 1066. Challacombe, the panhandle of Manaton parish, Devon, separated by moorland from the bulk of the parish, appears also to have been a separate estate in the medieval period. In each case we have an example of a feature which has been hinted at earlier, namely the composite estate structure of even some small parishes. Della Hooke's work on Anglo-Saxon charters in the west Midlands has demonstrated how Anglo-Saxon estates often consisted of blocks of land smaller than the later parishes (Hooke, 1981). The combining of such small building blocks to form parish territories could lie behind the irregularities of many parish boundaries whereby a settlement which 'naturally' would be expected to lie in one parish in fact forms a projection of another.

8. Medieval local government: county, hundred and wapentake

Tithing, vill and civil parish may be thought of as successive manifestations of a common entity, the basic grouping of people for the purposes of civil government. Above them rose a structure of administrative units through which the central institutions of government and justice reached down to every community in the land. These larger territorial groupings — the hundreds and their counterparts in eastern and northern England, the wapentake and ward, and, above them, the county or shire — form the subject of this chapter.

The county

The county or shire emerged in the late Anglo-Saxon period as the unit of administration with a direct link to central government, the sheriff (literally the 'shire-reeve') being the representative of royal authority in each shire. The counties into which England had been divided by 1200 remained more or less unchanged until the twentieth century, many county boundaries surviving intact until the major changes which came into effect in 1974. The county's administrative roles were financial, military and judicial. For financial purposes it was the principal unit for the gathering of taxes and other royal revenue; in military terms it was responsible, through the sheriff, for local defence; and it had a critical and long-standing role in the meting out of justice: each county had its court from the tenth century and, even when the Anglo-Saxon county courts were replaced by the itinerant assizes, these were still arranged on a county basis. With the exception of the counties palatine of Chester, Durham and, from 1351, Lancaster, distinguished by their quasi-autonomous governments, the counties of medieval England were similar institutions with the same responsibilities and relationship to the Crown and Parliament.

Despite their common function, however, the shires came into being through a long process of evolution across the centuries of Anglo-Saxon and Norman rule and different processes determined the laying out of their boundaries in different parts of the realm. The division of England into counties reflects the political geography of the Anglo-Saxon period, the three generations of county corresponding to the three principal political divisions at AD c.800: Wessex and the smaller southern English kingdoms; the great Midland kingdom of Mercia; and the northern kingdom of Northumbria, including those areas

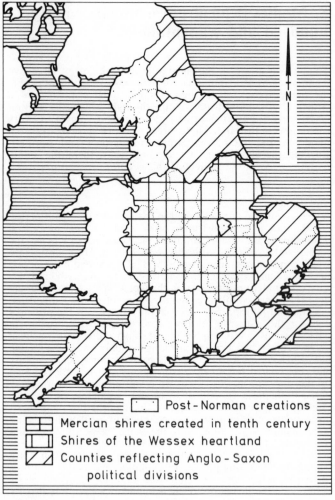

Figure 20. Origins of English counties.

west of the Pennines which were under Northumbrian influence at various times. Figure 20 is an attempt to portray these differences of origin.

The counties of southern England reflect the early Anglo-Saxon tribal and political groupings of the region. The relationship is most obvious in the south-east, where the early Saxon kingdoms of Sussex and Essex, the Jutish kingdom of Kent and the Anglian folk divisions of Norfolk and Suffolk (the northern and southern 'folk', respectively) each became a county. Likewise the counties of the far south-west, Devon and Cornwall, were based on the remnants of the pre-Saxon Celtic kingdoms of Dumnonia and Cornubia. In the heartland of Wessex the shire divisions had emerged by the middle of the ninth century, their names implying that they were folk areas governed from a central seat. 'Sumorsæte' means 'the people round Somerton'; 'Wiltunscir', the 'shire governed from Wilton'.

In the Midlands, by contrast, the counties appear to be deliberate artificial divisions made in the early eleventh century. With the exception of Rutland (a post-Conquest creation), all the Mercian shires take their names from their county town: Leicestershire is named from Leicester; Worcestershire from Worcester; Shropshire from Shrewsbury (it is recorded as 'Scrobbesbyrigscire' in 1006). The east Midland counties may have originated in the carving up of eastern Mercia between units of the Danish army when the Danelaw was established in the late ninth century. The west Midland shires, however, are thought to represent the deliberate creation of Wessex-style local government units in the decade or so after 1000, by carving the countryside up into territories with 'rateable values' of about 1200 or 2400 'hides', the 'hide' being the unit on which taxes and other obligations were assessed. The new pattern was independent of earlier folk divisions in the region: the new county of Shropshire, for example, combined parts of the territories of two quite distinct tribal groupings, the 'Wreocensætan', the 'settlers round the Wrekin', and the 'Magonsætan', a folk group living in northern Herefordshire and southern Shropshire (Taylor, 1957). The new counties may have been created by throwing together a number of smaller earlier units to reach the desired hidage. It has been suggested, for example, that Gloucestershire represents four earlier 'ferdings', including a short-lived shire based on Winchcombe (see Hill, 1981; Hooke, 1985). Despite being drawn to define deliberately created administrative territories, the boundaries of some of the Midland shires were extremely complex, with frayed edges and detached portions of one county lying in another, a pattern which survived until being tidied up by the Counties (Detached Parts) Act of 1844. One of the most complicated areas lay on the borders between Gloucestershire, Worcestershire and Warwickshire (see figure 23). Although it does not provide a complete explanation, the pattern of landownership in the eleventh century, particularly the estates of the church, goes some way to explain why settlements which naturally lay in Gloucestershire were accounted parts of Worcestershire, for example.

North of the Humber and the Mersey the medieval counties were Norman creations, though those east of the Pennines were based on erstwhile political divisions. Yorkshire was essentially the Danish kingdom of York; Northumberland and Durham represented the relict Anglo-Saxon kingdom of Northumbria. The counties of north-western England were new post-Conquest creations, made by putting together a number of ancient secular divisions. Westmorland, for example, consisted of Westmorland proper (the district west of the moors, that is the upper Eden valley north of Shap) together with the ancient territory of Kendale ('the valley of the Kent') and part of Lonsdale ('the valley of the Lune'). Lancashire was created by throwing together the remote western seaboard areas: the 'land between Ribble and Mersey' was formerly attached to Mercia; the ancient secular divisions north of the Ribble (Amounderness, part of Lonsdale, and Furness) had been part of Yorkshire and thus originally the kingdom of Northumbria. The creation of Cumberland in the 1170s (by uniting the 'land of Carlisle' with the ancient territory of Copeland) finally completed the division of England into counties.

Hundred and wapentake

Throughout England (with the exception of the four northern counties) a system of intermediate territories between county and vill or tithing had developed before the Conquest (figure 21). Termed 'hundreds' south of the Severn-Wash line and in the west Midlands, and 'wapentakes' in the east Midlands and Yorkshire, these districts emerged in the tenth century, primarily as judicial units, the hundred court being a district meeting, held every four weeks at a fixed meeting place, originally in the open air, and the hundred as a whole being responsible for pursuing criminals within its boundaries. In this respect hundred and tithing were parts of the same system. The hundred was also a taxation unit, the geld being collected hundred by hundred in the tenth and eleventh centuries. The terms 'hundred' and 'wapentake' throw some light on the origins of these units. The hundred probably originated, in theory at least, as a territory assessed at one hundred hides or as a police group consisting of one hundred families, while the term 'wapentake' is derived from the Scandinavian word *vapnatak* (literally 'weapon-take'), referring to the brandishing of weapons at a meeting of armed warriors when decisions were proclaimed by a clash of spears.

By comparison with the counties, the hundreds and wapen-takes were relatively unstable territories. Changes are recorded as early as the tenth century, when three Worcestershire hundreds were united to form a new hundred of Oswaldslow. In several counties (such as Shropshire and Warwickshire, for example) a reorganisation of hundredal boundaries took place after the Conquest so that we have to distinguish the Domesday hundreds inherited from before the Conquest from the hun-dredal pattern which applied for the rest of the middle ages. In Shropshire the reorganisation of the twelfth century left some hundreds little changed but completely remodelled other areas: Condover and Ford hundreds survived intact, though the latter changed its name (from 'Ruesset'), while the huge hundred of Bradford, covering the north-eastern quarter of the county, was

Figure 21. Intermediate divisions of English counties.

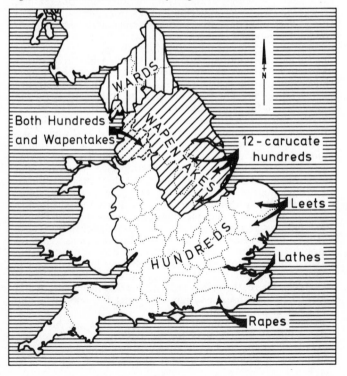

created by amalgamating the older hundreds of Wrockwardine and Hodnet. In the Norman period also holes in the hundredal patchwork were created by jurisdictional liberties — areas, usually corresponding to church or other extensive estates, which had their own systems of justice and did not have to send representatives to the hundred court. The pattern created by hundredal boundaries at a particular date was thus the result of changes since their inception as much as a reflection of conditions when they were first established.

The administrative functions of the hundred and wapentake as they emerged in the tenth century were essentially those of an institution born in Wessex which had been imposed on areas outside the Wessex heartland. Again we may ask what influences determined the grouping of settlements into hundreds. Unfortunately, there is no single or simple answer to this. In Wessex itself the hundreds often took their names from an ancient royal estate centre which lay at their core. In Somerset, for example, Crewkerne, Martock, Somerton and South Petherton hundreds were each centred on a pre-Conquest royal manor, though post-Conquest boundary changes severed the direct link between hundred and estate. In the west Midlands royal vills also gave their names to hundreds but many Mercian hundreds either appear to have been in origin early folk groups or bore names which recorded the district meeting place. In the first category fall the Shropshire hundreds of 'Mersete' ('the settlers on the boundary'), in the north-west of the county hard against Wales, and 'Ruesset' (the settlers round 'Rew'). In the second category fall a very large number of Midland hundred and wapentake names, many containing the elements *hlaw*, meaning a burial mound or barrow (for example Brinklow and Tremlow, Warwickshire; Munslow and Purslow, Shropshire; Blacklow and Botloe, Gloucestershire), 'tree' (for example Brimstree, Shropshire; Doddingtree, Worcestershire; Longtree, Gloucestershire; Wixamtree, Bedfordshire; Gartree, Leicestershire and Lincolnshire) or 'stone' (for example Bagstone, Dudstone and Tibblestone, Gloucestershire; Hurstingstone, Huntingdonshire). These barrows, lonely trees and distinctive boulders often lay on hilltops or road junctions at a convenient central point for the hundred meeting. In some cases the Midland hundreds appear to bear a relation to the landholding pattern of the late Saxon period; elsewhere, the names may suggest that the hundreds and wapentakes formalised a system of district folk moots, taking over their ancient meeting places.

In Yorkshire and Lancashire the wapentakes and hundreds were again closely related to the pattern of land tenure, particularly to the ancient compact estates embracing all the settlements in a district, known in the region as 'shires'. The pattern is particularly neat in south Lancashire, which contained great hundredal estates like Blackburnshire, Leylandshire and Salfordshire. Across the Pennines lay the wapentakes of Allertonshire, Howdenshire and Aldborough (earlier called 'Boroughshire') which, together with the wapentakes of Driffield, Gilling and Pocklington, each constituted a large royal estate in which outlying members 'lay to' an estate centre. Folk meetings were almost certainly a feature of these areas as well, and the Yorkshire wapentake name Skyrack (meaning 'shire-oak') is presumably akin to the tree names of hundreds further south (Barrow, 1973; Smith, 1961).

Other intermediate groupings

Hundreds and wapentakes covered all of England except the four northern counties but they were not the only territorial groupings between county and vill. The divisions of Yorkshire into three *ridings* (literally 'thirdings' or third parts) and of Lincolnshire into the three *parts* of Kesteven, Lindsey (itself divided into three ridings) and Holland continued to have administrative significance until 1974, but there were other groupings of vills which someone studying local boundaries will meet. As well as looking briefly at the intermediate divisions of the four northern counties, this section introduces some of the other territorial groupings which were found in medieval England.

Wards are found in place of hundreds or wapentakes in Northumberland, Durham, Cumberland and Westmorland. The term implies a defended or guarded unit but when and exactly why they were established is not known. They are first recorded in the thirteenth century but some, at least, appear to represent early territories akin to the 'shires' of Lancashire and Yorkshire. The Northumberland wards of Norhamshire and Islandshire were estates of great antiquity and the Cumberland wards of Copeland and Allerdale appear also to have been pre-Conquest entities. The four wards of County Durham may be rather different: it is striking how their boundaries converge in the vicinity of Durham city — a pattern which smacks more of deliberate planning than re-use of existing territories.

Lathes or *lests* were divisions of Kent which each contained two or more hundreds. They appear to pre-date the hundreds, which are thought to have been introduced in the mid tenth century, after Kent had been subsumed into Wessex. The lathes were more stable than the hundreds and probably represent the ancient *provinciae* or folk regions of the Kentish kingdom (Jolliffe, 1933).

Rapes were similar groupings of hundreds in Sussex. Though the term and some of the groupings may have been inherited from early district divisions of the South Saxon kingdom, it is now thought that the medieval pattern was remodelled, at least, in the decade after the Norman Conquest. Bramber rape, for example, bisects both hundred and deanery boundaries, suggesting that it was superimposed on the earlier administrative geography of the area (Cam, 1944).

Hundreds in Lincolnshire, Rutland and Nottinghamshire were different from those in other counties. The equivalent to the 'normal' hundred in those east Midland counties was, as we have seen, the wapentake. The hundred in these counties, recorded in Domesday Book, was a unit of assessment for taxation purposes containing twelve carucates. It appears to have been an artificial system imposed with reference neither to landholding patterns nor wapentake boundaries, probably in the tenth or eleventh century (Roffe, 1981).

Leets were small groupings of settlements for the purposes of geld collection recorded in Domesday Book for Norfolk and Suffolk, each hundred being composed of a number of leets (fourteen in South Greenhoe hundred, Norfolk, for example). It has been suggested that the East Anglian leets were pre-Conquest units, perhaps comparable to the small Danish twelve carucate hundreds of the east Midlands, discussed above. It is striking that some leets were described in the twelfth century as *villae integrae* ('complete vills'), the term discussed above in chapter 4 (Finn, 1967).

9. Ecclesiastical administration: diocese and deanery

Parishes do not exist in a vacuum; they are the bottom rung of a ladder of organisation which, before the Reformation, led up to St Peter's successor, the Pope. The nested hierarchy of parishes grouped into rural deaneries, which were in turn grouped into archdeaconries, which were themselves subdivisions of dioceses, created a set of boundary patterns which were both comparatively stable and preserved in their outlines memories of other ancient territorial groupings in the countryside.

The diocese

While the parish priest exercised spiritual authority over his parish, a bishop ruled over a much larger territory, the *diocese* or *see*. The parishes within a diocese were bound to the diocesan seat by the bishop's prerogatives of institution (the placing of a parson, usually nominated by someone else — the patron of the parish — in a living made vacant by death or transfer), confirmation of church membership, and general oversight of spiritual and ecclesiastical matters through the process of visitation (by which the churchwardens of each parish were required to report on the physical upkeep of the church and the moral and spiritual health of the inhabitants). Just as the existence of territorial liberties created jurisdictional holes in the county and hundred, however, so the diocese could be peppered with ecclesiastical *peculiars*, parishes in which the powers normally exercised by the bishop were held by someone else, often the bishop of another diocese.

From the mid twelfth century to the Reformation England was divided into seventeen dioceses (see figure 22). The medieval pattern was modified in 1541-2 by the creation of the five sees of Bristol, Chester, Gloucester, Oxford and Peterborough, and a more radical reshaping took place in the mid nineteenth-century reformation of the Church of England's administration. The pattern of diocesan boundaries that remained stable from the twelfth century to 1541 came into being as the result of a long process of evolution, stretching from the establishment of the see of Canterbury, usually dated to AD 597, to the creation of the see of Carlisle in 1133.

The earliest diocesan divisions reflected the political geography of Anglo-Saxon England and parts of the post-Conquest pattern thus incorporate ancient political boundaries. The first generation of sees came into being as Christianity spread to the various independent kingdoms of seventh-century England. The

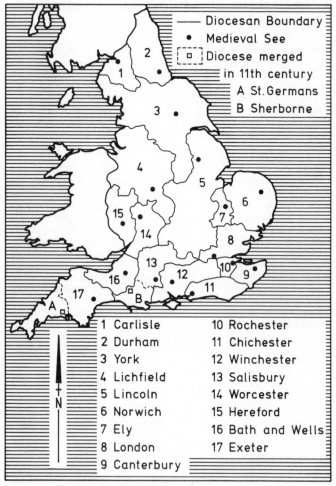

Figure 22. The dioceses of medieval England.

see of Canterbury (created AD 597) was co-terminous with the kingdom of Kent; London (created 604) with the kingdom of the East Saxons; Winchester (founded about 635 at Dorchester-on-Thames and transferred in the 660s) was the see for Wessex;

Lichfield (early seventh-century) was the Mercian see, and York (established 625) that of the kingdom of Northumbria. In the seventh century these primary sees were subdivided on the creation of new dioceses. Rochester was carved out of Canterbury in 604, and a major subdivision of the Mercian bishopric took place under Bishop Seaxwulf (675-91): the new Midland dioceses of Hereford, Worcester, Leicester and Lindsey reflected the tribal divisions of Mercia, the best known relationship being that of the diocese of Worcester, created in 679 to serve the sub-kingdom of the Hwicce. The medieval boundaries of Worcester and the neighbouring see of Hereford preserved these ancient tribal boundaries and bore little relationship to the later pattern of county boundaries which dated, as we have seen, from the tenth or early eleventh century (see figure 23). Other early subdivisions along political or tribal lines occurred in East Anglia, where the primary see was divided in 673 between Dunwich (for the southern folk division) and Elmham (for the northern folk), and in the carving of the diocese of Selsey out of Winchester in 709 to serve the kingdom of Sussex. The slightly earlier division of the West Saxon see in 705 appears to have been determined by topography, the new see of Sherborne taking control of all Wessex west of Selwood.

A further phase of reorganisation took place in the late ninth and early tenth century. Two processes can be identified: first, the disruption of the existing pattern of diocesan organisation in the Danelaw and, second, the reorganisation of episcopal administration in Wessex. The result of the disruption in the Danelaw was a reduction in the number of sees in eastern England when diocesan organisation was re-established in the mid tenth century. The dioceses of Leicester, Lindsey and Dunwich all disappeared from the map. In Wessex the pattern of diocesan organisation was made to conform to the area's division into counties in 909: new sees were created at Crediton, Wells and Ramsbury to serve Devon, Somerset and Wiltshire/Berkshire respectively, leaving the see of Sherborne to coincide with Dorset and that of Winchester to serve Hampshire and Surrey.

The final stages in the evolution of the medieval pattern took place after the Conquest. In 1075 Archbishop Lanfranc ordered the removal of the bishops' seats from villages to towns, resulting in changes in the location of the seats and, hence, the name of the see, while the diocesan boundaries remained unchanged. Thus the ancient see of Sherborne (which had been united with Ramsbury in 1058) was removed to Old Sarum; Wells moved to Bath; Selsey to Chichester; Elmham first to Thetford and then, in 1094, to Norwich; and Dorchester-on-Thames (which had become the successor to the Mercian sees of Lindsey and

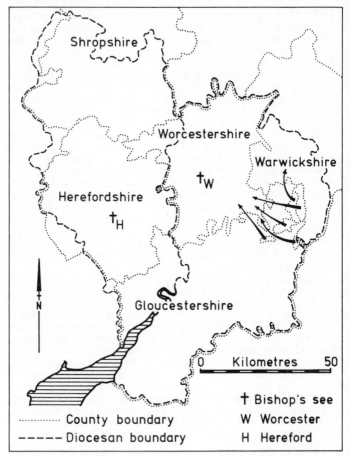

Figure 23. Diocesan and county boundaries, Hereford and Worcester dioceses.

Leicester) to Lincoln. Finally, the see of Ely was created in 1109 to cover Cambridgeshire and the Isle of Ely, and the diocese of Carlisle in 1133 to cover the 'land of Carlisle' which had been annexed to England in 1092 and had formerly been included within the see of Glasgow.

Because of the very long process of evolution which lay behind the pattern of medieval dioceses, it is not possible to explain the grouping of parishes into different dioceses in terms of any single determinant. The boundaries of some sees pre-dated the creation of counties and reflected early political or tribal divisions. Worcester and Hereford fall into this category, as do Carlisle (reflecting political divisions before the creation of the medieval counties of the north-west) and Chichester (where both diocese and county were determined by the ancient kingdom of the South Saxons). Other dioceses, notably those of Wessex, post-date the counties and were created to coincide with the secular units.

The archdeaconry and rural deanery

Between the bishop and the parish priest were two intermediate levels of ecclesiastical jurisdiction, the archdeacon and the rural dean. The archdeacon was the bishop's chief administrative officer, to whom much routine work was delegated and who acted as 'the bishop's eye' in bringing the state of the diocese to the bishop's notice. The rural dean was a lesser official whose principal duty was to supervise the work of a group of parish priests and the upkeep of their churches and other buildings. Although it is an oversimplification, the archdeacon was in general responsible for an area comparable in size to a county and the rural dean for a group of parishes of the same size as many hundreds or wapentakes. The origins of both offices in England are not fully understood but both patterns of organisation appear to have evolved in the late eleventh or twelfth century, are recorded in the *Taxatio Ecclesiastica* of 1291 and remained stable until the Reformation.

At both levels there was a contrast between northern and eastern England on the one hand, where archdeaconries and deaneries often corresponded to units in the secular local government hierarchy, and western England on the other, where such a correspondence was rare. Archdeaconries in the north and east coincided with counties. The diocese of Durham contained two, created in the early twelfth century, one responsible for Northumberland, the other for County Durham. In York diocese the archdeaconries corresponded to the ridings of Yorkshire, while the seven archdeaconries of the vast diocese of Lincoln mirrored the seven counties it embraced. In contrast, the south-western dioceses of Bath and Wells and Exeter, each covering a single county, were both divided into three archdeaconries (Thompson, 1943).

A similar contrast was exhibited by the rural deaneries (see figure 24). They bore a close relationship to the hundredal divisions throughout eastern England from Essex through East Anglia and the east Midland counties to Yorkshire. In Cumbria and Lancashire there was again a close relationship between civil

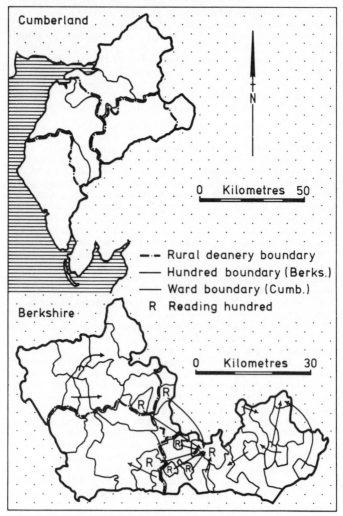

Figure 24. Contrasting relationships between rural deaneries and hundredal units.

and ecclesiastical units, deaneries corresponding quite closely to the wards of Cumberland and Westmorland and the large compact hundreds of Lancashire. An interesting exception is Lonsdale deanery, which covered a compact area, arguably an ancient secular territory consisting, as its name indicates, of the valley of the Lune. Its ten constituent parishes were carved up between the three counties of Westmorland, Yorkshire and Lancashire when the county boundaries were drawn in the twelfth century.

In southern and western England, from Kent through Wessex and into the west Midlands, there was little correspondence between deanery and hundred and deaneries generally took their names from one of the parishes within their bounds. Two factors have been identified behind the grouping of parishes into deaneries in these areas. The first is the pattern of land tenure, notably the influence of monastic estates. The deanery of the Vale of Evesham appears to have corresponded to the central estates of Evesham Abbey as they were before the Conquest (Cox, 1975), and a similar relationship seems to explain the deanery of Wenlock (Shropshire), which covered the estates of St Milburga's monastery at Much Wenlock. A second factor in determining deanery boundaries may have been the residual influence of early minster church territories. It has been suggested, for example, that the deaneries of Clun, Burford and Pontesbury in Hereford diocese not only took their names from early minsters but also embraced territories which had been dependent on those mother churches at an early date.

10. Parish boundaries in Scotland and Wales

One of the themes in the history of England's administrative landscape is that many of the institutions, and a substantial legacy of local territorial boundaries, date from the late Anglo-Saxon and Norman periods. Scotland and Wales were outside the sphere of influence of the Anglo-Saxon kings; the imposition of 'Norman' institutions began rather later than in England; and large areas of both countries retained their native cultures until well into the middle ages. Scotland remained an independent nation until the union of 1707 and its legal system and established church remain separate and fundamentally different from their English counterparts. Wales, partially subjugated by the English Crown in the thirteenth century, was formally united with England in 1535 and subsequently had English administrative institutions imposed upon it. In both countries, therefore, the parish developed in a context quite different from that in England and this chapter briefly outlines the salient features of parish development in Scotland and Wales.

The parish in Scotland

The Scottish administrative landscape contained nothing directly comparable to the townships or tithings of medieval England. Their place was taken by the barony (a unit of lordship and landownership roughly the same as the English manor) for the purposes of taxation and the administration of justice in the medieval period. Rural settlements tended to be small hamlets, termed 'townships' or 'fermtouns', several of which would be found in even a small barony. The division of the land surface between Scottish townships inevitably created a pattern of boundaries on the ground, but these were in general of no administrative significance beyond the internal management of the estate. Overlying the pattern of medieval landownership was a network of ecclesiastical parish boundaries as in England and, again as in England, the parish gained civil responsibilities after the Reformation. In Scotland the parish kirk sessions were responsible from 1579 for poor relief, and they also acquired responsibility for the management of schools and the registration of christenings, marriages and burials, for example. As its responsibility grew, the parish tended to replace the barony as the principal unit of local administration, post-medieval taxation and the nineteenth-century censuses taking the parish as the basic unit of territorial organisation.

If one of the dominant influences in the development of the territorial landscape of England was the expansion of the kingdom of Wessex in the tenth century, the equivalent influence in Scotland was the long slow process by which the kings of Scots gained control of the whole of modern Scotland between the twelfth and fifteenth centuries. Indeed, the persistence of other cultural influences — Gaelic in the western Highlands, Norse in Caithness and the Northern Isles — well into the middle ages resulted in the preservation of quite distinct territorial patterns in different parts of the kingdom. The origins of the parish in Scotland may be thought of as falling into three distinct regional patterns.

First was the heartland of the Scottish kingdom in the lowlands of central eastern Scotland together with those areas to the north (Aberdeenshire and Moray, for example) and south-west (Galloway and Ayrshire) which were brought under Scottish control in the twelfth and thirteenth centuries. In these areas subjugation to the kingdom of Scots was accompanied by the spread of feudal land tenure. The development of the parochial system in southern and eastern Scotland bore similarities to its evolution in England. When documentary sources become available in the twelfth century there is evidence for the existence of early mother churches, akin to the English minsters, served by groups of clergy and often originating as early monasteries. The churches of Whithorn and Kirkcudbright in Galloway and Stobo and Old Jedburgh further east were of this type, the latter two continuing to possess large parishes containing dependent chapels. Churches served by similar groups of clergy, sometimes termed 'culdees' (literally 'followers of God') or 'scolocs' ('scholars'), were also scattered up the eastern lowlands from Fife to Aberdeenshire. There are hints that bishops and Celtic landowners had founded new churches before the spread of feudalism in the twelfth century, but it is clear that a vigorous phase of church planting took place in the twelfth century as new landowners founded churches to serve their estates. The edict of David I (1124-53) making the payment of tithes compulsory served to fix parochial boundaries and it is striking that many parishes coincided with a feudal barony. As in England, the payment of tithe tended to fossilise parish boundaries as the patron and rector of existing churches resisted the creation of new parishes which would decrease their income. Some new parishes were created during the thirteenth century, however, often where a larger barony was subdivided into smaller units of lordship (Cowan, 1961).

The pattern of parochial development was rather different in the Gaelic west. There the influence of the Celtic church remained strong, and the physical geography of the western Highlands and islands in many places fragmented the limited areas suitable for settlement into small pockets hemmed in by mountains and the sea. The numerous place-names containing the prefix Kil- (from the Gaelic *cill,* 'a cell or church') reflect the existence of numerous church sites, many dedicated to early Celtic saints, and were probably coined by the ninth century. By no means all of these cells evolved into parish churches in the medieval centuries but several of the Western Isles possessed many more parish churches before the Reformation than they did afterwards.

The development of parishes in the Scandinavian Northern Isles was different again. Under Norwegian control until 1468, the two groups of islands together formed the diocese of Orkney, which fell within the archdiocese of Trondheim and thus looked away from Scotland altogether. In both Orkney and Shetland medieval ecclesiastical organisation consisted of numerous chapels, each serving a small township community, which were grouped into parishes, which were themselves grouped into 'priest's districts' (*prestegjeld*). The pattern seems to have been imposed by the joint authority of earl and bishop in the eleventh century and in Orkney appears to represent an artificial division of each island into parishes, which were then grouped into priest's districts. In Shetland, on the other hand, the pre-existing pattern of secular administration was made use of, the regional 'thing areas' (the communities meeting at the local assembly or 'thing') coinciding with the priest's districts, which were the principal units of ecclesiastical organisation, the parish having a more shadowy existence (Cant, 1984).

When we turn to the post-medieval period, the history of the Scottish parish is again rather different from its counterpart south of the border. The parish was freed from episcopal control by the Reformation and, gathering civil functions, the pattern of parish boundaries in Scotland was subject to a considerable degree of change. Indeed, Scottish parish churches, no longer the consecrated sites that they were before the Reformation, have been much more liable to changes in location than those south of the border, particularly in the century after 1750, when so much of the rural settlement pattern of Scotland was rewritten during the agricultural revolution.

Two very different areas will illustrate the extent of post-medieval change. The first is lower Annandale (Dumfriesshire), where the net effect was a reduction in the number of parishes between the early fourteenth century and the eighteenth (see figure 25). Some small parishes, like Brydekirk, Kirkconnel and Irving, had been swallowed up by larger neighbours before the Reformation, probably during the troubled and impoverished fourteenth and fifteenth centuries. But much of the change was the result of deliberate reorganisation: Hoddom parish was expanded by the incorporation of the parishes of Luce and

Ecclefechan in 1609, and Great and Little Dalton were united in 1633. Just to the east of the area covered by figure 25 a complete reorganisation took place in 1703, when two new parishes were created: Eskdalemuir, carved out of Westerkirk, and Langholm, made by combining the ancient parishes of Staplegorton, Wauchope and Half Morton.

The isles of Mull, Ulva and Iona (figure 26) provide a second example. In the medieval period they contained seven parish churches and at least six chapels, two of which were supported by their own teinds (tithes) and were thus almost of parochial status. There were also ten other places bearing names incorporating the element *cill-* (for example Kilbrenan, Kilmoluag), many of which were burial grounds serving isolated communities. At the Reformation the seven medieval parishes were thrown into a single parish of Mull. Then, in 1688, the island was divided into two parishes, and the southern one was itself subdivided about forty years later.

Figure 25. Lower Annandale, Dumfriesshire: medieval and post-medieval parishes.

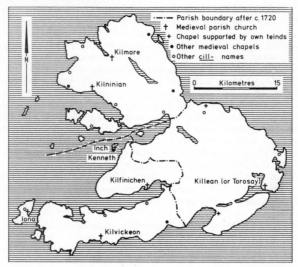

Figure 26. Isle of Mull: parochial history.

Not all of Scotland experienced such a degree of parochial reorganisation, some areas of the lowlands and eastern Scotland retaining the medieval pattern almost unchanged. However, in addition to the wholesale uniting and division of parishes in the nineteenth century many new parochial divisions were created for religious purposes which left the older parochial pattern untouched for civil purposes. Such 'ecclesiastical' parishes are referred to as parishes *quoad sacra* ('for sacred purposes only'). As in England, the parish boundary pattern was tidied and simplified in the later nineteenth century. The Local Government (Scotland) Act of 1889 appointed commissioners to rationalise county and parish boundaries and they turned their attention to the 134 parishes which contained detached portions and simplified the boundary pattern (Shennan, 1892).

The parish in Wales

The history of the administrative landscape of Wales is very different from that of both England and Scotland. On the one hand Wales had a strong native system of territorial organisation which survived the pressure from English institutions during the middle ages and, indeed, was adopted by the Normans; on the other hand the 1535 Act of Union with England imposed the English system of counties and hundreds on the country.

The native civil administrative system which bound Celtic

society together for the collection of rents and dues and the administration of justice consisted of a nested hierarchy. At the top was the *cantref* (literally 'one hundred townships'), which was divided into two or more commotes (*cymydau*) which functioned as the principal units for the collection of dues and holding of courts. Commotes were in turn divided into *gwestfas* or *maenors* for the collection of rents (originally taking the form of food renders and giving the *gwestfa* — 'a feast' — its name), each of which was composed of several *trefi* or 'townships'. In the scattered settlement pattern of medieval Wales a *tref* often embraced several hamlets but it was the basic unit for the assessment of dues. After the union with England, though nomenclature was changed and the English system of hundredal organisation was imposed, elements of the native medieval territorial pattern survived. The new hundreds were very often reincarnations of one or more commotes. In Caernarvonshire the medieval commotes were taken almost unchanged to form the new hundreds; in Carmarthenshire and Glamorgan there was a greater degree of reorganisation with commotes being re-grouped and sometimes divided to create hundreds of similar size, but even in these counties long sections of the hundred boundaries followed those of the older units (Richards, 1969). The *tref,* already rendered *villa* or *villata* in Latin documents, came to be translated as 'township' in English and survived as a basic unit of civil administration into the nineteenth century.

Where, then, does the parish fit into the tight and persistent system of secular territorial organisation? The origins of the Welsh parish mirror the early development of parishes in England and Scotland. Once again there is a distinction between early mother churches served by groups of clergy and later lesser churches achieving parochial status in the century after the Norman Conquest. In Wales the earliest churches were Celtic monastic institutions, known as 'clas' churches, run by a community (*clas*) of canons under an abbot or bishop. Like the Anglo-Saxon minsters and the 'culdee' churches of eastern Scotland, the monastic mother churches of Wales probably served large, but possibly ill defined, territories.

It was not until after the Norman conquest of Wales that the Welsh church came fully under the leadership of Rome and that the system of dioceses and parishes was established. Norman bishops were appointed to St David's, Llandaff and Bangor in the early twelfth century, each representing the elevation of an ancient 'clas' church into a bishop's seat. The diocese of St Asaph was created in 1143 and it is generally thought that territorial parishes came into being at about this time. The relationship between the new parishes and the secular territorial hierarchy has received comparatively little attention and it is difficult to gain a clear picture of the processes which underlay the pattern of parish boundaries in medieval Wales. However, the subject has been studied to some extent in the province of Gwynedd in North Wales. There it has been suggested that both parish and township boundaries were laid out in the twelfth century as a result of deliberate action by the secular and ecclesiastical powers. Colin Gresham has argued that a systematic reorganisation of the pattern of landholding and civil administration under the native king Owain Gwynedd (died 1170), which led to the establishment of township boundaries, coincided with the laying out of parish boundaries by the newly established diocesan authorities (Gresham, 1987).

The Tudor legislation giving parishes responsibility for highways and poor relief affected Wales as well as England and undoubtedly encouraged the parish to take over the secular role of the *tref*. The western seaboard counties of Anglesey, Caernarvonshire and Pembrokeshire contained numerous small parishes which, by the nineteenth century, had superseded the townships as the basic units of civil administration. In the hill country of the Welsh heartland, however, the parishes were larger and, like their counterparts in northern England, were divided for secular purposes into townships or 'hamlets', which were the descendants of the medieval *trefi*.

11. Further reading

The Victoria County Histories

A wealth of detailed accurate information about the development of parish and township boundaries, the pattern of lordship, and the history of local government is contained in the rather forbidding red volumes of the *Victoria History of the Counties of England* (the *VCH*). Where they have been published, the topographical volumes contain detailed histories of every parish, while the general volumes, which treat subjects on a county-wide basis, include useful articles on ecclesiastical organisation for most counties, and the development of local government for some.

General reference works

Successive editions of the *Ordnance Survey Six-Inch (1:10,560)* and *Twenty-five Inch (1:2500) maps* and the published *Census Reports* have been mentioned already as indispensable sources for establishing the boundaries of administrative units before the local government reforms of the past century, and for charting boundary changes since the middle of the nineteenth century. They may be supplemented by the following useful works of reference:

Booth, J. R. S. *Public Boundaries and the Ordnance Survey 1840-1980.* Ordnance Survey, 1980. Provides a useful outline of the statutes affecting parish and other boundaries.

Cowan, I. B. *The Parishes of Medieval Scotland.* Scottish Record Society, Edinburgh, 1967. An alphabetical listing of all parishes in existence before 1560.

Richards, M. *Welsh Administrative and Territorial Units: Medieval and Modern.* Cardiff, 1969. A detailed listing of all units with maps of medieval commotes, post-medieval hundreds and modern local government areas.

Shennan, H. *Boundaries of Counties and Parishes in Scotland as Settled by the Boundary Commissioners under the Local Government (Scotland) Act, 1889.* William Green, Edinburgh 1892. Gives the texts of orders made by the Commissioners and explanations of boundary changes thus made, including details of places transferred from one parish to another.

Youngs, F. A. *Guide to the Local Administrative Units of England I: Southern England.* Royal Historical Society, 1979. Lists all recorded parishes, townships, tithings etc in counties south of the Severn-Wash line, with dates of alterations in their boundaries and details of the superior administrative units in which they lay.

Other general works

The following general works include useful discussions and/or maps of parishes and other units of local administration:

Hill, D. *An Atlas of Anglo-Saxon England.* Blackwell, 1981.

Jewell, H. M. *English Local Administration in the Middle Ages.* David and Charles, 1972.

McNeill, P., and Nicholson, R. (editors). *An Historical Atlas of Scotland c.400-c.1600.* Conference of Scottish Medievalists, St Andrews, 1975.

Pollock, F., and Maitland, F. W. 'Jurisdiction and the Communities of the Land' in *The History of English Law,* volume I, pages 527-688. Cambridge University Press, second edition, 1923.

Rees, W. *An Historical Atlas of Wales from Early to Modern Times.* Faber, second edition, 1972.

Stenton, F. M. *Anglo-Saxon England.* Clarendon Press, third edition, 1971.

Local, regional and specialised studies cited in the text
Addleshaw, G. W. O. *The Beginnings of the Parochial System.* St Anthony's Hall Publications, York, 1953.

FURTHER READING

Addleshaw, G. W. O. *The Development of the Parochial System from Charlemagne to Urban II*. St Anthony's Hall Publications, York, 1954.

Aldsworth, F. G. 'Parish Boundaries on Record', *The Local Historian*, 15 (1982), pages 34-40.

Aston, M. (editor). *Aspects of the Medieval Landscape of Somerset*. Somerset County Council, 1988.

Barrow, G. W. S. *The Kingdom of the Scots*. Arnold, 1973. Especially chapter 1, 'Pre-feudal Scotland: Shires and Thanes'.

Beresford, M. W. 'A Journey along Boundaries' in *History on the Ground*, pages 25-62. Alan Sutton, 1984.

Bettey, J. H. *Church and Parish: a Guide for Local Historians*. Batsford, 1987.

Bonney, D. J. 'Two Tenth-century Wiltshire Charters Concerning Lands at Avon and at Collingbourne', *Wiltshire Archaeological and Natural History Magazine*, 64 (1969), pages 56-64.

Bonney, D. J. 'Early Boundaries in Wessex' in P. J. Fowler (editor), *Archaeology and the Landscape*, pages 168-86. Baker, 1972.

Bonney, D. J. 'Early Boundaries and Estates in Southern England' in P. H. Sawyer (editor), *Medieval Settlement*, pages 72-82. Arnold, 1976.

Cam, H. M. *Liberties and Communities in Medieval England*. Cambridge University Press, 1944.

Campbell, J. 'The Church in Anglo-Saxon Towns' in D. Baker (editor), *The Church in Town and Countryside*, pages 119-35. Blackwell for the Ecclesiastical History Society, 1979.

Cant, R. G. 'Settlement, Society and Church Organisation in the Northern Isles' in A. Fenton and H. Pálsson (editors), *The Northern and Western Isles in the Viking World*, pages 169-79. John Donald, 1984.

Costen, M. D. 'Rimpton in Somerset: a Late Saxon estate', *Southern History*, 7 (1985), pages 13-24.

Cowan, I. B. 'The Development of the Parochial System in Medieval Scotland', *Scottish Historical Review*, 40 (1961), pages 43-55.

Cox, D. C. 'The Vale Estates of the Church of Evesham, *c.*700-1086', *Vale of Evesham Historical Society Research Papers*, 5 (1975), pages 25-50.

Finn, R. W. *Domesday Studies: the Eastern Counties*. Longman, 1967.

Fishwick, H. (editor). *Pleadings and Depositions in the Duchy Court of Lancaster, 1485-1558*. Record Society of Lancashire and Cheshire, 1896.

Gelling, M. 'Boundaries and Meeting Places' in *Signposts to the*

Past: Place-names and the History of England, pages 191-214. Dent, 1978.

Goodier, A. 'The Formation of Boundaries in Anglo-Saxon England: a Statistical Study', *Medieval Archaeology*, 28 (1984), pages 1-21.

Gresham, C. A. 'Medieval Parish and Township Boundaries in Gwynedd', *Bulletin of the Board of Celtic Studies*, 34 (1987), pages 137-49.

Hooke, D. *Anglo-Saxon Landscapes of the West Midlands: the Charter Evidence*. British Archaeological Reports, 1981.

Hooke, D. *The Anglo-Saxon Landscape: the Kingdom of the Hwicce*. Manchester University Press, 1985.

Hoskins, W. G. *Fieldwork in Local History*. Faber, 1967.

Jolliffe, J. E. A. 'The Origin of the Hundred in Kent' in J. G. Edwards *et al.* (editors), *Historical Essays in Honour of James Tait*, pages 155-68. Manchester, 1933.

Lees, B. A. 'The Statute of Winchester and Villa Integra', *English Historical Review*, 41 (1926), pages 98-103.

MacDermot, E. T. *The History of the Forest of Exmoor*. David and Charles, 1973.

Peterken, G. F. *Woodland Conservation and Management*. Chapman and Hall, 1981.

Pool, P. A. S. 'The Tithings of Cornwall', *Journal of Royal Institution of Cornwall*, new series 8 (1981), pages 275-337.

Rackham, O. *The History of the Countryside*. Dent, 1986.

Roberts, B. K. *The Making of the English Village*. Longman, 1987.

Roffe, D. 'The Lincolnshire Hundred', *Landscape History*, 3 (1981), pages 27-36.

Rogers, A. J. 'Parish Boundaries and Urban History: Two Case Studies', *Journal of British Archaeological Association*, third series 35 (1972), pages 46-64.

Smith, R. B. *Blackburnshire: a Study in Early Lancashire History*. Leicester University Press, 1961.

Sylvester, D. 'Church and Countryside' in *The Rural Landscape of the Welsh Borderland*, pages 164-89. Macmillan, 1969.

Taylor, C. *Village and Farmstead: a History of Rural Settlement in England*. George Philip, 1983.

Taylor, C. S. 'The Origin of the Mercian Shires', in H.P.R. Finberg (editor), *Gloucestershire Studies*, pages 17-51. Leicester University Press, 1957.

Tupling, G. H. 'The Pre-Reformation Parishes and Chapelries of Lancashire', *Transactions of Lancashire and Cheshire Antiquarian Society*, 67 (1957), pages 1-16.

Unwin, T. 'Townships and Early Fields in North Nottinghamshire', *Journal of Historical Geography*, 9 (1983), pages 341-6.

FURTHER READING

Warner, P. 'Shared Churchyards, Freemen Church Builders and the Development of Parishes in Eleventh-century East Anglia', *Landscape History,* 8 (1986), pages 39-52.

Williams, J. H. 'Northampton's Medieval Parishes', *Northamptonshire Archaeology,* 17 (1982), pages 74-84.

Williamson, T. 'Parish Boundaries and Early Fields: Continuity and Discontinuity', *Journal of Historical Geography,* 12 (1986), pages 241-8.

Winchester, A. J. L. 'The Medieval Vill in the Western Lake District: Some Problems of Definition', *Transactions of Cumberland and Westmorland Antiquarian and Archaeological Society,* 78 (1978), pages 55-69.

Winchester, A. J. L. *Landscape and Society in Medieval Cumbria.* John Donald, 1987. Especially pages 13-36 ('Lordship and Territory').

Appendix: place-names recording boundaries

Some of the place-name elements which record the presence of territorial boundaries have been mentioned in the previous chapters. This list draws together a range of such elements and gives examples of names derived from each. Most of the words noted here are discussed in detail in A. H. Smith's *English Place-Name Elements* (English Place-Name Society, volumes 25 and 26, Cambridge, 1956). The abbreviation OE indicates that the word is Old English.

calenge (Middle English): 'challenge, dispute', e.g. Callans Wood (Worcestershire).

ceast (OE): 'strife, contention', e.g. Chesland (Wiltshire); Chest Wood (Essex).

crioch (Gaelic): 'a boundary', e.g. Allt na Creiche ('boundary burn'), Isle of Mull, on the boundary between Iona and Kilvickeon parishes.

devise (Old French): from Latin *divisa,* ' division, a boundary', e.g. Devizes (Wiltshire); Viza, Vizacombe (Devon).

ecg (OE): 'an edge'. Usually used of a hill scarp but in some minor names refers to places near a boundary, e.g. Nedge Hill, on the boundary between Shifnal and Stirchley parishes (Shropshire); Edge, Reagill township (Westmorland), on the boundary between Crosby Ravensworth and Morland parishes.

flit (OE): 'strife, dispute', e.g. Flitteridge (Sussex).

fyn (Welsh, Cornish): 'end, boundary', e.g. Ffinnant (Montgomery), Naphene (Cornwall), both meaning 'boundary valley'.

grima (Old Norse): 'mark or blaze on a tree to denote a boundary', e.g. Leagram (Lancashire) ('road or track with a *grima*').

har (OE): 'grey, hoary'. Because of its frequent use in 'hoarstone' (see chapter 6), it seems also to have come to mean 'boundary' as in Harden (Yorkshire West Riding) ('*har*-valley'), which lies on a wapentake boundary, and Harrold (Bedfordshire) ('*har*-wood') on the county boundary with Northamptonshire.

land-gemære (OE): 'land boundary', e.g. Landermere (Essex); Laundimer Woods (Northamptonshire).

land-scearu (OE): 'landmark, boundary, share of land' e.g. Lancercombe (Devon); Launcherley (Somerset).

mære (OE): 'a boundary, border'. Often the name of a boundary stream, as in Merebrook, Merebeck, Mereburn. In Merridge (Somerset) the second element is 'ridge'; in Merbach (Herefordshire) it is 'valley'.

mearc (OE): 'boundary', e.g. Marden (Wiltshire), Marsden (Gloucestershire, Yorkshire West Riding) ('boundary valley'); Marksbury (Somerset) ('boundary fortification', probably referring to the Wansdyke); Chilmark (Wiltshire) ('boundary marked by posts or poles').

rá (Old Norse): 'land-mark, boundary', e.g. Raby (Durham); Roby (Lancashire), both meaning 'settlement on a boundary'.

rán (OE), **reinn** (Old Norse): both mean 'a boundary strip or balk' and are used of divisions in open fields. In some examples they appear to refer to territorial boundaries, e.g. Ranmore (Surrey), which is on a parish boundary, and Rainworth (Nottinghamshire) ('boundary ford') which is on a wapentake boundary.

rima (OE): 'rim, edge, border', e.g. Rimpton (Somerset); Ryme (Dorset), both close to the county boundary.

scead (OE): 'separation', used in the sense of 'boundary', e.g. Shadwell (several examples).

skial (Old Danish): 'boundary', e.g. Skeldike (Lincolnshire) ('boundary ditch'); Skelfleet (Yorkshire East Riding), ('boundary creek').

tæcels (OE): 'a boundary mark or boundary', e.g. Tachbrook (Warwickshire), the boundary between the dioceses of Lichfield and Worcester.

teo (OE): 'a boundary' e.g. Teffont (Wiltshire) ('boundary spring'); Tyburn (Middlesex), formerly *merfleote*, 'boundary creek'.

terfyn (Welsh). 'a boundary', e.g. Tarvin (Cheshire).

threap (OE): 'a dispute, contention', e.g. Threapland, Threapwood. See chapter 6.

Index